STANLEY HALL

***Front Cover:* NEAR TYNE YARD 1 August 1984**
The Leeds-Edinburgh HST set after being derailed on a set of trailing points at Tyne Yard. *BR*

***Back Cover:* POLESWORTH 21 July 1947**
The streamlined engine of the down Liverpool express is being rerailed. The tender and the first two coaches are seen still lying on their sides. *Duncan Claridge Collection/IAL*

***Previous page:* PADDINGTON 23 November 1993**
No 50041 *Bulwark*, the damaged locomotive of the Penzance sleeper, stands upright again in Paddington station. It appears to have survived the high speed derailment very well. *M. Roberts/IAL*

First published 1997

ISBN 0 7110 2549 5

Published by Ian Allan Publishing

an imprint of Ian Allan Ltd, Terminal House, Station Approach, Shepperton, Surrey TW17 8AS.
Printed by Ian Allan Printing Ltd at its works at Coombelands in Runnymede, England.

Code: 9711/D

Contents

Preface

This book gives details of the more serious or significant accidents which happened on four of the principal main lines of the railways in Britain during the 20th century. The main lines selected are:

London Euston to Glasgow Central (the West Coast main line);
London King's Cross to Edinburgh Waverley and Glasgow Queen Street (the East Coast main line);
London Paddington to Penzance (the Great Western main line);
London Waterloo to Exeter Central (the South Western main line).

Whilst the selection of accidents is bound to be somewhat subjective, the West Coast main line heads the list with 60, followed by the East Coast main line with 50, which is probably a fair representation of traffic levels on those two routes. The Great Western has 20, with none west of Aller Junction, and the South Western has 11, with none west of Salisbury.

In the accidents listed, no passenger was killed in any train accident in the 20th century on the West Coast main line between Winwick Junction, north of Warrington, and Mossband, just north of Carlisle, a distance of 122 miles, which is a remarkable record.

As might be expected, the preponderance of accidents is in the London suburban area, with 12 on the West Coast main line in the first 22 miles, eight on the East Coast main line in the first 21 miles, nine on the Great Western main line in the first 23 miles, and seven on the Southern in the first 15 miles. Of the nine accidents since 1980, five have occurred on the Great Western. There have been none on the East Coast since 1957 — a fine record.

A large number of simplified track layouts and signalling diagrams have been included in order to clarify the text, but these are only schematic and intended as a guide. They do not necessarily represent the actual track and signalling configurations.

Railway historians, particularly those who study accidents, owe a great debt to the Inspecting Officers of the Railway Inspectorate for the wealth of reliable detail, track layouts, signalling plans, etc in their published accident reports. Books such as this one would not be possible without access to those reports, and I wish to record my gratitude to the Inspectorate. I am also grateful to the National Railway Museum, York, for allowing me to use their reading room for research purposes over many days.

Analysis of Times, Dates and Causes of Accidents

The Time of Day

12am	5 accidents	12pm	3
1am	4	1pm	3
2am	8	2pm	3
3am	5	3pm	6
4am	2	4pm	9
5am	8	5pm	9
6am	6	6pm	11
7am	4	7pm	5
8am	5	8pm	6
9am	3	9pm	6
10am	6	10pm	6
11am	4	11pm	7

Average: 5.5 accidents per hour
(Not all times are recorded)

There were only 12 accidents in the morning peak 7am to 10am, but 29 in the evening peak 4pm to 7pm. The quietest period was 12 noon to 3pm, with only nine accidents. There have been far fewer night-time trains in recent years.

The Day of the Week

Sunday	16 accidents
Monday	21
Tuesday	10
Wednesday	29
Thursday	18
Friday	22
Saturday	23
Average:	20 per day

There is no apparent explanation for Tuesday's low figure nor for Wednesday's high figure. Strangely, half of the Great Western line's accidents took place on a Wednesday — 10 out of 20. Many of Sunday's accidents had some connection with permanent way engineering work.

The Month of the Year

January	13 accidents	July	17
February	8	August	14
March	8	September	15
April	7	October	10
May	12	November	12
June	12	December	13
Average:	approx 12 per month		

The spring figures are remarkably light. The high summer figures probably represent additional summer holiday and excursion trains. The autumn figures are no more than average, which seem to indicate that long dark nights and the prevalence of fog did not unduly influence the figures.

The Causes

Driver Error	accidents
Signals passed at danger (no ATC/AWS)	34
Signals passed at danger (AWS ineffective)	5
Too fast over fast/slow junctions	6
Other excessive speed	11
Signalman's error, two trains in a section, etc	16
Faulty track	15
Mechanical faults	17
Fire on train	7
Obstruction (loads falling off or displaced, etc)	4
Miscellaneous errors by drivers, signalmen, fitters, guards, shunters, inspectors, etc	26

AWS and modern signalling controls would have prevented almost half of the accidents.

Today's railway is very safe, and passengers are further safeguarded by the greatly improved crash-worthiness of modern coaches.

1 — WEST COAST MAIN LINE

EUSTON TO GLASGOW CENTRAL

EUSTON STATION
7.53am Saturday 26 April 1924

Location: Euston No 4 signalbox up slow line.

The 7.15am electric multiple-unit from Watford to Euston, running at 20-30mph under clear signals, crashed into the rear of the 5.30am Cup Final excursion from Coventry to Euston, which was standing at Euston No 4 signalbox up slow line home signal. Although all the coaches of the excursion train were gas-lit, there was no fire.

Cause: Signalman's error. The signalman at Euston No 4 signalbox had just dealt with an up Scotch express on the up fast line, but he sent the 'Train out of Section' signal for that train to Camden No 1 signalbox on the up slow line block instrument in error. He was then offered, and accepted, the 7.15am EMU from Watford, resulting in the collision.

Formation: The Watford train was a six-car EMU.

Casualties: Five passengers were killed and 68 were injured.

Signalling: Absolute block. There were no track circuits at Euston No 4 up home signals. The signalbox had an electrically operated miniature lever frame.

Possible safety measures: A track circuit at the up slow line home signal, with appropriate signalling controls, would have prevented the accident.

WILLESDEN JUNCTION
8.55am Monday 5 December 1910

Location: Willesden Junction station up slow line platform No 4.

The 8.30am passenger train from Watford to Broad Street, running under clear signals at 20mph, crashed into the rear of the 8.27am passenger train from Watford to Euston, which was standing in Willesden Junction station.

Cause: Signalman's error. A trainee signalman at the signalbox in the rear, Willesden Junction No 5, who was clearing the signals for another train, pulled off the up slow line home signal in error, thus allowing the 8.30am train to proceed.

Formations: *The 8.27am from Watford* (a side tank engine and 10 50ft bogie vehicles).
The 8.30am from Watford (a side tank engine and seven bogie vehicles).

Damage: The last two vehicles of the 8.27am were wrecked, the last one being telescoped.

Casualties: Five passengers were killed and 146 were injured, several seriously.

Signalling: Absolute block, semaphore signals.

Possible safety measures: An electric lock on the home signal at No 5 signalbox, requiring a 'line clear' from No 2 signalbox, would have prevented the signal from being cleared.

WILLESDEN JUNCTION
11.6pm Friday 4 July 1969

Location: Up slow line at trailing connection with up goods loop, in advance of signal WN96, 150yd on London side of Milepost 5¾.

The 22.13 electric multiple-unit (EMU) passenger train from Bletchley to Euston, running under clear signals, collided with a wrecked buffer stop. It had been thrown on to the line a few seconds earlier by an empty parcels train which had been running on the adjoining up goods loop when it passed the outlet signal at danger and ran into the buffer stop at about 25mph.

Cause: Signal passed at danger by the driver of the empty parcels train.

Formation: The passenger train was formed by two four-car Class AM10 EMUs.

Damage: The first six cars of the passenger train were derailed.

Casualties: Minor.

Signalling: Track circuit block, colour-light signalling. No AWS at the outlet signal from the up goods loop (WN102). Controlled from Willesden Junction power signalbox.

Possible safety measures: There had been two previous similar accidents at this location and it was decided to remove the goods loop altogether.

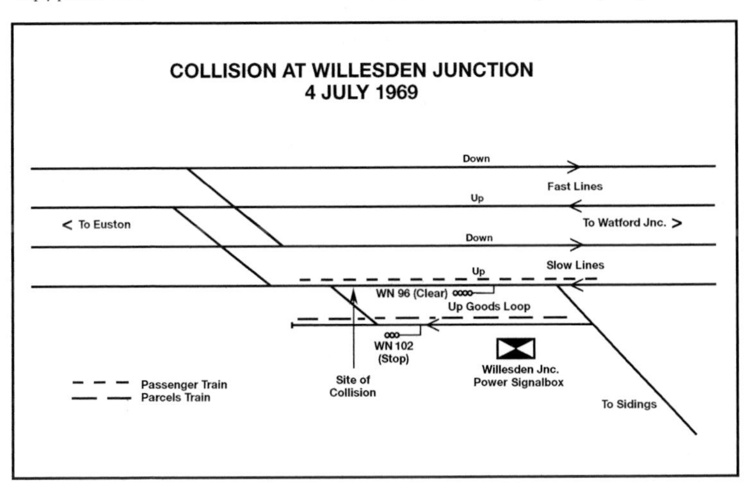

WEMBLEY
6.4pm Thursday 11 October 1984

Location: Down slow line, at trailing connection with up and down goods line, 409yd beyond signal WN27 controlled by Willesden Junction power signalbox, and about 100yd south of Wembley Central station.

The 17.54 electric multiple-unit passenger train from Euston to Bletchley ran past a signal at danger and came into sidelong collision at just under 60mph with the 11th wagon of a freightliner train which was just crossing onto the down slow line from a goods line.

Cause: The driver of the passenger train failed to observe or respond properly to signal WN27 which was displaying a red aspect and to the preceding

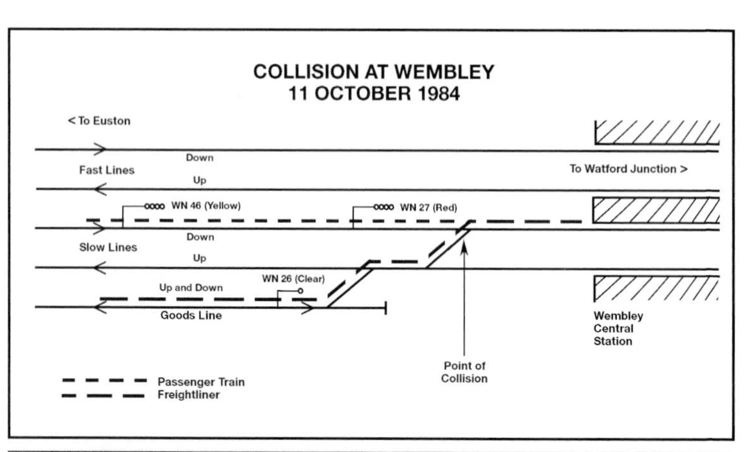

WEMBLEY 11 October 1984
Looking south from Wembley Central station. The first two coaches have been turned upright and drawn forward. ***Mick Roberts/IAL***

signal WN46 displaying a yellow aspect. Such accidents occur when drivers allow their attention to wander, but in this case a distinguished panel of medical experts, having examined the driver, concluded that, on the balance of probabilities, the driver's behaviour was due to a rare but well-recognised medical condition which resulted in an episode of amnesia and confused behaviour due to a transient disturbance of blood flow in the posterior cerebral arteries.

Formation: The passenger train: two four-car Class 310 EMUs.

Damage: The leading two cars were overturned on to their sides, and all the following cars, except the last one, were derailed.

Casualties: Three passengers were killed and a number were injured, two of whom were detained in hospital.

Signalling: Track circuit block with four-aspect colour-light signalling and AWS. Controlled from Willesden Junction power signalbox.

Possible safety measures: This type of accident would be prevented by an automatic train protection system which checks that the driver is actually responding to an adverse signal by reducing the train's speed, and would interpose if he failed to do so.

WEMBLEY STATION
7.10pm Saturday 12 October 1940

Location: Up fast line at the north end of the platform.

The 11.50am express passenger train from Liverpool Lime Street to Euston, running at about 55mph under clear signals, struck a heavily loaded four-wheeled luggage barrow which had run back down the platform ramp and stopped foul of the up fast line.

Cause: The barrow had overpowered the porters who were attempting to push it up the ramp.

Conditions: Dusk.

Formation: 'Patriot' class 5XP 4-6-0 No 5529, 11 corridor coaches and two four-wheeled vehicles.

Damage: The engine and tender, and the first seven vehicles, were derailed. Rescue work took place during a red alert air raid warning and the normal lighting which would have been used during peacetime could not be allowed. It had to be done using handlamps and torches.

Casualties: Nine passengers and the two enginemen were killed. Four passengers had serious injuries.

Possible safety measures: Better supervision of cross-line barrow movements and provision of a parcels lift. However, this was a wartime accident, involving relatively inexperienced platform staff.

HARROW AND WEALDSTONE
8.19am Wednesday 8 October 1952

Location: Harrow and Wealdstone station, up fast line platform.

The 8.15pm express passenger train from Perth to Euston passed the Harrow No 1 signalbox up fast line outer and inner home signals at danger, and ran into the rear, at between 50 and 60mph, of the 7.31am local passenger train from Tring to Euston, which was standing at the up fast platform. A few moments later, the 8am express passenger train from Euston to Liverpool Lime Street and Manchester London Road, which had passed the down fast line distant signal in the clear position and was running at about 60mph, crashed into the wreckage of the two trains. The local passenger train had approached Harrow on the up slow line, but had then been crossed over to the up fast line for a fast run to Euston.

Above: **HARROW AND WEALDSTONE 8 October 1952**
'Princess Royal' class Pacific No 46205 Princess Victoria on an up express passes the exact point where the first collision occurred. ***IAL***

Cause: Signals passed at danger by the 8.15pm from Perth. There had been drifting patchy fog, and the fog signalling regulations had been applied earlier, but at 8.10am, 9min before the accident, the fog had cleared sufficiently for normal working to be resumed. The fog signalling regulations are applied when the signalman is unable to see for more than 200yd and require a fog signalman to be on duty at the outer home signal if normal acceptance is to be maintained. There had been no fog signalman on duty and in those circumstances the signalman was not allowed to accept a train on the up fast line with a train standing at the up fast line platform. A fog signalman was not required at the up fast line distant signal because it was a colour-light signal. It is not known why the 8.15pm from Perth failed to stop at the up fast line outer home signal, because both enginemen were killed in the crash. The signalman had worked correctly in accordance with his regulations.

Formations: *8.15pm from Perth* — 'Princess Coronation' class 8P 4-6-2 No 46242 *City of Glasgow*, with 11 bogie vehicles, marshalled milk van, brake van, four corridor coaches, four sleeping cars, brake van. There were about 85 passengers in the train.
7.31am from Tring — Class 4MT 2-6-4 tank

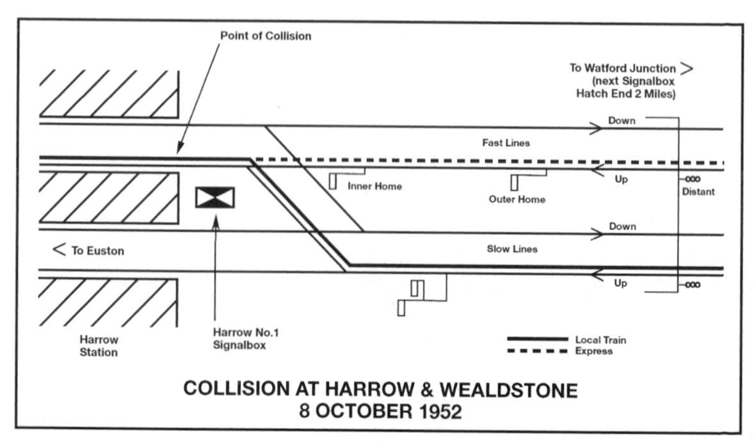

e: **HARROW AND WEALDSTONE 8 October 1952**
ching for survivors in the mass of tangled wreckage. ***IAL/Keystone Press***

No 42389, with nine non-corridor coaches. There were about 800 passengers in the train. *8am Liverpool and Manchester* — Pilot engine 'Jubilee' class 6P 4-6-0 No 45637 *Windward Islands*, and train engine 'Princess Royal' class 8P 4-6-2 No 46202 *Princess Anne*, with 11 corridor coaches and four brake vans in rear. There were about 200 passengers in the train.

Damage: The last three coaches of the local train were telescoped into the length of one coach. The first five vehicles of the Perth train piled up behind and above its overturned engine. Both engines of the down express turned over on to their sides and the first eight coaches were wrecked.

Casualties: 108 passengers and four enginemen were killed, and in addition 157 injured passengers were conveyed to hospitals, where 84 were detained, many with serious injuries. There is evidence that 64 passengers were killed in the local train, 23 in the Perth train and only seven in the down express. The other 14 were not located, but may have been on the platform. This was the worst collision in terms of deaths in peacetime in the whole history of Britain's railways, and it has not been surpassed since. The worst collision took place at Quintinshill, near Gretna, in 1915 (see later pages).

Signalling: Absolute block with semaphore signals and colour-light distants on the up lines.

Possible safety measures: Automatic warning control would almost certainly have prevented this accident, and the Railway Executive was already carrying out the trials which resulted in the adoption of the automatic warning system (AWS).

BUSHEY
8.40pm Saturday 16 February 1980

Location: 180yd south of Bushey station.

The 20.25 express passenger train from Euston to Manchester Piccadilly was travelling on the down fast line at just below 100mph when the leading coach became derailed.

Cause: A broken welded joint in the left-hand rail.

Formation: Electric locomotive No 87007 and nine coaches, Mk 1, 2 and 3. There were about 150 passengers in the train.

Damage: The locomotive was not derailed, but ran forward with the first two coaches still coupled to it but derailed. The next three coaches overturned on to their sides on the dc electrified lines, whilst the remaining four coaches remained upright, though derailed.

Casualties: There were no fatalities, but 48 passengers were taken to hospital, where 19 of the more seriously injured were detained.

Possible safety measures: Better training and supervision of welders.

WATFORD JUNCTION
10.30pm Thursday 23 January 1975

Location: Up and down fast lines near bridge 61 (a viaduct), at 16 miles 1,519yd.

Just as the 19.10 express passenger train from Manchester Piccadilly to Euston was accelerating along the up fast line from the Watford stop it ran into some steel stillages which had fallen from a freight train. The leading locomotive became derailed foul of the down fast line on which the 22.15 sleeping car express from Euston to Glasgow was approaching at about 85mph. The locomotive of the sleeping car express struck the derailed locomotive corner to corner and was deflected down a steep embankment, pulling most of the train into derailment.

Cause: The freight train from which the stillages had fallen was the 20.12 'Company Train' No 6M50 from Dagenham to Halewood, conveying car parts loaded in 17 pallet vans, and it was thought that it

Above: **WATFORD JUNCTION 23 January 1975**
Looking northwards along the Glasgow sleeper, with the wrecked locomotive of the up Manchester express alongside. *IAL*

had been interfered with by potential thieves whilst it was standing at signals at Gospel Oak. They had left a door unsecured, and it had opened during the journey, allowing stillages to fall out.

Formations: *The 19.10 up express (1A81)* — electric locomotives No 83003 leading and No 86204, with 12 vehicles, airbraked. The train conveyed 52 passengers.
The 22.15 down sleeper (1S18) — electric locomotive No 86209 and 14 vehicles, marshalled guard's brakevan, three sleeping cars, eight Mk 1 coaches and two guard's brakevans. Vacuum braked.

Damage: *Train 1A81* — severe damage to locomotive No 83003.
Train 1S18 — the locomotive came to rest on its side at the foot of an embankment, followed by the front guard's brakevan. The following coaches as far as the 10th were derailed, two of them leaning dangerously.

Casualties: The driver of train 1A81 was killed and three staff needed hospital treatment. Eight injured passengers were detained in hospital.

Possible safety measures: BR took steps to provide steel raves within the door openings of pallet vans to prevent stillages from accidentally rolling out.

Above: **WATFORD JUNCTION 23 January 1975**
The locomotive of the Glasgow sleeper plunged down the embankment, followed by the leading vehicle. ***IAL***

WATFORD JUNCTION
5.24pm Thursday 8 August 1996

Location: Watford South Junction, approx. 200yd north of signal WJ759.

The 17.04 electric multiple-unit (EMU) from Euston to Milton Keynes, travelling on the down slow line, passed signal WJ759 at danger and collided sideways-on with an empty EMU which was being crossed from the up slow line to the up fast line across the down slow line.

Cause: The driver of the 17.04 passed a signal at danger.

Formations: *The passenger train* — one four-car EMU.
The empty stock train — two four-car EMUs.

Damage: The leading car of the passenger train was overturned on to its side.

Casualties: One passenger was killed and 15 people were taken to hospital and detained.

Signalling: Multiple-aspect colour-light signalling with continuous track-circuiting and AWS.

Controlled from Watford power signalbox.

Possible safety measures: Automatic train protection or similar.

WATFORD JUNCTION
5.7pm Wednesday 3 February 1954

Location: Up fast line in Watford Tunnel.

The up 'Royal Scot' 10am Glasgow to Euston was travelling through Watford Tunnel at about 65mph when a broken rail derailed the last pair of wheels of the eighth coach.

Cause: The rail broke at the end due to a corrosion fatigue crack developing, following heavy blows in earlier years when there was a lower level of maintenance.

Formation: 'Princess Coronation' Class 8P 4-6-2. No 46250 *City of Lichfield* and 10 coaches.

Damage: The train ran on at virtually unchecked speed for about 1½ miles until the derailed wheels hit the points and crossings at Watford No 2 signalbox, whereupon the last two coaches became completely derailed. They broke away from the remainder of the train and came to rest leaning against the platform at Watford station just as the 4.37pm Euston to Wolverhampton express was leaving. The sides of some of its coaches were grazed as they scraped past the two derailed coaches. The first eight coaches of the 'Royal Scot' were brought to a stand when the brakes were automatically applied by the parting of the train.

Casualties: No one was seriously injured.

Track: 109lb flat bottom rail, laid new in November 1950. The standard of track maintenance in the tunnel was considered to be generally good.

Above: **WATFORD JUNCTION 3 February 1954**
An up Liverpool express is seen leaving Watford Tunnel behind 'Princess Royal' class Pacific No 46207 *Princess Arthur* of Connaught on 14 April 1952. *J. C. Flemons/IAL*

KING'S LANGLEY
Friday 8 August 1969

Location: Immediately south of King's Langley station.

A wagon in freight train No 6Z48 from Liverpool and Wolverhampton to Ripple Lane became derailed on the up slow line, and a Motorail train from Perth to Kensington Olympia on the up fast line ran into the wreckage at high speed.

Cause: The load in the wagon had not been properly secured and it shifted in transit, causing the wagon to derail about two miles north of King's Langley. All four lines were blocked when following wagons became derailed.

Formations: *The Motorail train* — electric locomotive No E3129, three coaches and 'cartic' (articulated car-carrying) vehicles.

The goods train — electric locomotive No E3069 and 25 open wagons, each loaded with three coils of strip steel, 2½ to 5 tons in weight, secured open end upwards to pallet boards. Six wagons had been detached at various places en route with hot axlebox, damaged floor or shifted load.

Damage: *The Motorail train* — the locomotive, three coaches and the leading 'cartic' wagon were derailed.
The freight train — several wagons were overturned.

Casualties: None.

Possible safety measures: Improved loading and securing of strip steel in coils.

KING'S LANGLEY
11.9pm Wednesday 13 March 1935

Location: 200yd north of Milepost 22, opposite the 'Railway Arms'.

The 4.55pm express meat train from Alexandra Dock to Broad Street failed in section on the up fast line between Nash Mills and King's Langley signalboxes. The train had just restarted, when it was run into at the rear at about 25mph by the 5.50pm milk train from Stafford to Euston, which had entered the section under clear signals. The wreckage spilt over on to the down fast and slow lines and moments later the 10.30pm partially fitted freight train from Camden to Holyhead, running at about 40mph on the down slow line, crashed into the wreckage. This resulted in the up slow line being blocked and a few seconds later a coal train, running on that line at 25-30mph, also ran into the wreckage.

Cause: An error by the signalman at King's Langley, who concluded that the meat train had passed him, and thereupon wrongly sent the 'Train out of Section' signal to Nash Mills. He was then in a position to accept the milk train, which he did.

Formations: *The meat train* — 'Claughton' class 4-6-0 No 5946, with 42 fitted wagons and brakevan.
The milk train — Class 4 compound 4-4-0 No 1165,with 22 fitted milk tanks and vans.
The freight train — 'Patriot' class 5XP 4-6-0 No 5511, with 45 wagons and brakevan.
The coal train — Class 7F 0-8-0 No 9598, with 70 wagons and brakevan.

Damage: *The meat train* — the rear four wagons and brakevan were thrown across the down fast line.
The milk train — the engine and 11 tanks/vans were derailed, some being piled up.
The freight train — the engine was derailed and 14 wagons were derailed and smashed.
The coal train — the engine and 20 wagons were derailed, some being piled up.

Casualties: The driver of the milk train was run down and killed by the freight train as he set off to protect the line. The guard of the meat train and the fireman of the coal train were injured.

Signalling: Absolute block, with semaphore signals.

Possible safety measures: A form of 'lock and block' to ensure that a second 'line clear' could not be given until the preceding train had actually arrived at or passed King's Langley.

Above: **KING'S LANGLEY 13 March 1935**
'Patriot' class 4-6-0 No 5511, the engine of the Camden to Holyhead freight, stands derailed after ploughing through a pile of wrecked and derailed vehicles. ***Hulton-Deutsch***

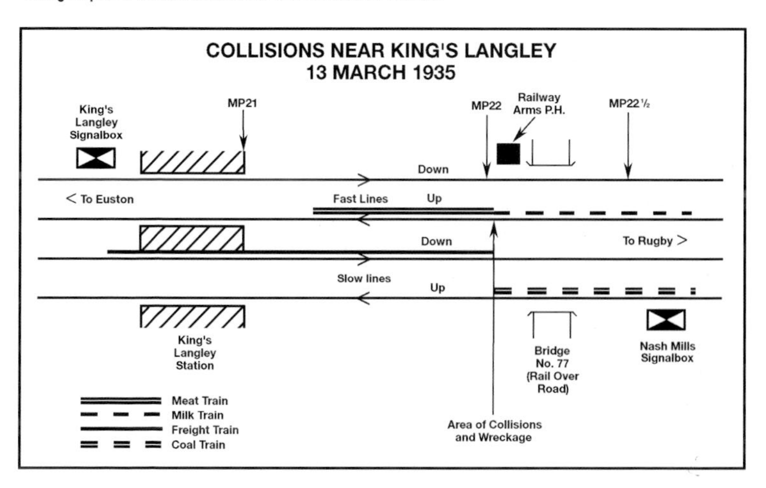

BOURNE END
9.3am Sunday 30 September 1945

Location: Bourne End signalbox, at the crossovers between the fast and slow lines. Near Milepost 26.

Engineering work was in progress on the fast lines in Watford Tunnel, and up trains were being diverted to the up slow line at Bourne End through a 20mph crossover. The 8.20pm sleeping car express from Perth to Euston failed to reduce speed and became derailed when passing through the crossover at between 50 and 60mph.

Cause: The driver failed to reduce speed. It is not known why.

Conditions: Daylight, with low sun.

Formation: 'Royal Scot' class 4-6-0 No 6157 *The Royal Artilleryman* and 15 coaches. There were 398 passengers, including 42 in sleeping cars.

Damage: The engine turned over on to its side and plunged down a 9ft embankment, taking the first coach and the third to seventh coaches with it. They piled up into a heap of wreckage. The second coach was thrown on to its side across the lines. The last three coaches remained on the rails.

Casualties: 41 passengers lost their lives, plus the driver and fireman. A total of 64 passengers were detained in hospital for more than a week. This was the worst peacetime disaster in England up to that time.

Signalling: Absolute block with semaphore signalling and colour-light distants. When the junction was set from the up fast line to the up slow line the distant signal displayed two yellows as an indication of that fact to the driver. The clearance of the outer and inner home signals was not delayed.

Possible safety measures: AWS would have warned the driver of the caution signal. A different method of operating the signals, so that the home signals were maintained at danger until the speed of the train had been reduced, might have been effective, but only if the driver had observed and obeyed them. After this accident the LMS abandoned the special two-yellow indication for junction working at distant signals. They were the only railway company to have adopted it.

Above: **BOURNE END 30 September 1945**
'Royal Scot' class 4-6-0 No 46156 *The South Wales Borderer* passes Bourne End on the down fast line on a down Workington express on 27 August 1955. The train concerned in the accident was being diverted from the up fast line (next to the down fast line) to the up slow line (extreme left) through the points in the centre of the photograph. Note that the signals for this movement are on the right-hand side of the lines.
R. M. Newland/IAL

LEIGHTON BUZZARD
12.20pm Sunday 22 March 1931

Location: Leighton Buzzard No 1 signalbox fast line to slow line crossover just south of the station.

Trains on the down fast line were being diverted at Leighton Buzzard to the down slow line owing to engineering work ahead. The 11.30am express passenger train from Euston to Glasgow and Edinburgh, travelling at 55mph, was derailed whilst making this movement.

Cause: The driver failed to reduce speed for the 20mph turnout. He also passed the junction home signals at danger.

Conditions: Bright and sunny.

Formation: 'Royal Scot' class 4-6-0 No 6114 *Coldstream Guardsman* and 14 bogie vehicles. The train conveyed 183 passengers and 20 dining car and other railway staff.

Damage: The engine and tender were overturned. The first three coaches were destroyed and the fourth damaged. The fifth to the tenth coaches were derailed and suffered some damage.

Casualties: Three passengers, the driver and fireman, and a dining car cook were killed. Three passengers and two railway employees were injured and detained in hospital.

Signalling: Absolute block and semaphore signals. The down fast line distant signal had two arms, one for the down fast line and one for a movement from the down fast line to the down slow line. The signalman had set his junction facing points from the down fast line to the down slow line, as he was entitled to do, but he did not clear his signals because he saw the train approaching at high speed.

Possible safety measures: AWS would most probably have prevented this accident.

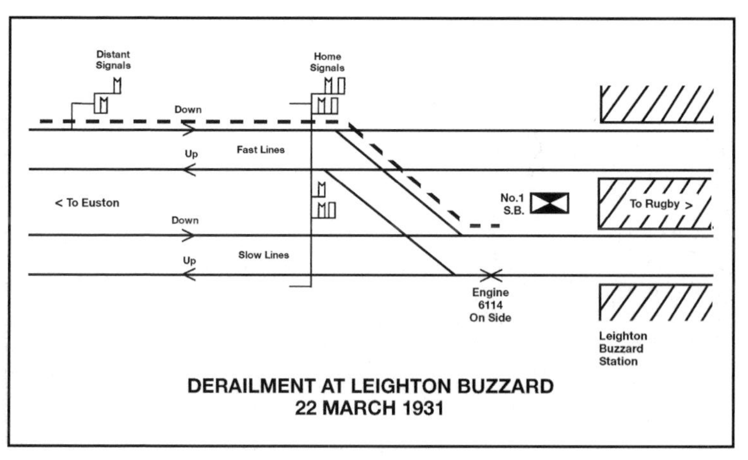

DERAILMENT AT LEIGHTON BUZZARD
22 MARCH 1931

LINSLADE TUNNEL
2am Thursday 9 December 1982

Location: Down slow line at the north end of the tunnel, north of Leighton Buzzard.

Train 1S18, the 22.55 sleeping car express from Euston to Glasgow, travelling at normal speed under clear signals, became derailed whilst emerging from the tunnel.

Cause: About half an hour earlier a freight train had passed on the adjoining up fast line, and a rail crossing assembly, part of a consignment of permanent way material being conveyed on the train, had become displaced. It struck the north portal of the tunnel and fell on to the down slow line, to be struck by train 1S18. The wagon had been irregularly shunted over the hump at Toton despite such movements being prohibited.

Formations: *Train 1S18* — electric locomotive No 81016 and 14 vehicles, marshalled two guard's brakevans, five sleeping cars, six coaches and a guard's brakevan. Buckeye coupled and vacuum braked.
The freight train 6M86, 16.50 'Speedlink' Healey Mills to Willesden — electric locomotive and 12 airbraked vehicles, maximum speed 60mph.

Damage: Train 1S18 — the locomotive bounced off the tunnel wall and collided violently with a bridge pier, before coming to rest 330yd beyond the tunnel mouth. Twelve vehicles were derailed but remained upright and in line.

Casualties: The driver was killed, and another driver and a passenger were injured.

Possible safety measures: Improve the loading and securing methods and the inspection arrangements of such consignments.

BLETCHLEY
8.53pm Friday 13 October 1939

Location: Down fast line at the south end of the station.

The 7.37pm from Euston to Inverness was standing in the station. A van was being attached to the rear by a shunt engine when it was run into by the 7.50pm Euston to Stranraer at about 45mph. The Stranraer train was booked to stop at Bletchley.

Cause: The Stranraer train passed Bletchley No 1 outer and inner home signals at danger. It was also running too fast to have been able to stop in the station.

Conditions: Dark and raining. There was a blackout in force, obscuring landmarks which drivers used to locate themselves.

Formation: *The Stranraer train* — Class 5P5F 4-6-0 No 5025 (pilot engine) and 'Royal Scot' class 4-6-0 No 6130 *The West Yorkshire Regiment* (train engine) with 11 vehicles.

Damage: The collision took place chimney to chimney with former LNW 0-8-0 No 9169, which was thrown on to the down fast platform, demolishing the refreshment and waiting rooms and part of the roof.
The Inverness train — the last three vehicles (all vans) were destroyed.
The Stranraer train — both engines were derailed, and the leading vehicle was derailed and damaged.

Casualties: A passenger, a porter and a postman were killed. Five passengers and the driver of the

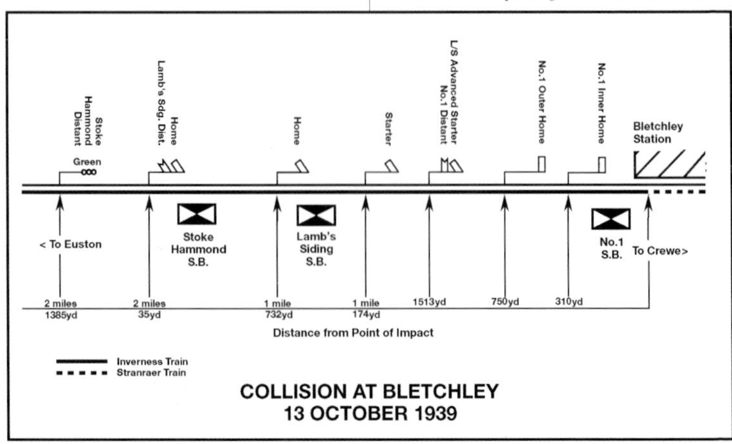

COLLISION AT BLETCHLEY
13 OCTOBER 1939

0-8-0 were seriously injured. The driver of engine No 5025 was tried for manslaughter, but the judge directed the jury and a 'not guilty' verdict was returned.

Signalling: Absolute block, with semaphore signalling. Bletchley No 1 down fast line distant signal was a semaphore signal underneath the starting signal at the previous signalbox, Lamb's Siding.

Possible safety measures: AWS would most probably have prevented this accident.

WEEDON
9.55am Saturday 14 August 1915

Location: Between Stowe Tunnel and Weedon, near Weedon No 2 down distant signal and Milepost 69.

The double-headed second portion of the 8.30am Irish Mail Euston to Holyhead, travelling at about 60mph, became derailed.

Cause: The right-hand coupling rod of the engine of the 8.45am express passenger train from Birmingham to Euston, 'George the Fifth' 4-4-0 No 1489 *Wolfhound*, came adrift and pushed out of alignment the track of the adjoining line on which the Irish Mail was approaching. A new split pin had been put in at Rugby, but the jaws may not have been properly opened.

Formation: Irish Mail — 'Precedent' class 2-4-0 No 1189 *Stewart* (pilot engine) and 'Renown' class 4-4-0 No 1971 *Euryalus*, with15 vehicles, including seven which were gas-lit.

Damage: Neither engine overturned, but the first three vehicles, all vans, went down an embankment. The next four vehicles, all coaches, went down an embankment on the up side, the third one being telescoped broadside by the fourth.

Casualties: 10 passengers were killed and 21 were injured, some severely.

Track: 90lb 60ft rails.

Possible safety measures: More care in maintenance.

WEEDON
11.15am Friday 21 September 1951

Location: South of Stowe Hill Tunnel.

The 8.20am express passenger train from Liverpool Lime Street to Euston became derailed whilst travelling at 60 to 65mph.

Cause: A defect in the engine bogie. The leading axleboxes were tight in the horn guides.

Formation: 'Princess Royal' class 4-6-2 No 6207 *Princess Arthur of Connaught* and 15 bogie vehicles.

Damage: The engine landed on its side down a 12ft embankment. The third and fourth coaches were virtually destroyed, whilst the next five were scattered amongst the wreckage.

Casualties: Seven passengers and a dining car attendant were killed and seven passengers were fatally injured. A total of 26 passengers and nine dining car staff were injured.

Track: Bull-headed rails. The derailed bogie wheels smashed the chairs, allowing the track to break up.

Possible safety measures: Improved maintenance and supervision.

Above: **WEEDON 21 September 1951**
Rerailing No 6207 on 28 October, over five weeks after the accident. *T. G. Wassell*

NUNEATON
1.54am Friday 6 June 1975

Location: Down fast line, near the south end of Nuneaton station.

The 23.30 sleeping car express from Euston to Glasgow failed to reduce speed when approaching Nuneaton for a permanent way speed restriction of 20mph, and entered the speed-restricted area at about 80mph. It was derailed.

Cause: The driver did not see the warning boards for the speed restriction because the lights had gone out, and he wrongly assumed that the speed restriction had been taken off. He did not reduce speed. The propane gas supply to the lights had run out, and the automatic changeover valve to a second gas bottle had been isolated.

Conditions: Dark but clear.

Formation: Electric locomotives Nos 86006 and 86242 (not under power), bogie brakevan, five sleeping cars, buffet car, seven sleeping cars, bogie brakevan (15 vehicles).

Damage: Extensive. The first locomotive continued forward and remained upright, the second one mounted the platform. The first four sleeping cars were scattered, mainly in zigzag fashion and on their sides. The following coaches remained coupled and more or less in line. Only the last vehicle was not derailed.

Casualties: Two passengers and two sleeping car attendants were killed, and two more passengers died in hospital. Ten people were detained in hospital with serious injuries. The driver was charged with manslaughter, but after a three-day trial he was found not guilty and discharged.

Possible safety measures: The use of a permanent AWS magnet at speed restriction warning boards was introduced as a result of this accident and speed restriction signs were improved.

Below: **NUNEATON 6 June 1975**
The derailed coaches of the sleeping car express were flung in all directions at the south end of the station.
IAL

POLESWORTH
10.38am Monday 21 July 1947

Location: Near Milepost 105¼, south of Polesworth station.

The 8.30am express passenger train from Euston to Liverpool Lime Street was travelling at about 65-70mph under clear signals on the down fast line near Polesworth, when it became derailed.

Cause: Defective track. The track on the curve at the site of the accident was not fit for traffic of the prevailing speed or weight. Among the defects, there was insufficient holding power of the screw fastenings of the chairs in the 18-year-old sleepers.

Formation: 'Princess Coronation' class 4-6-2 No 6244 *King George VI*, and 16 bogie vehicles.

Damage: The engine overturned and the two leading vehicles also overturned and were wrecked. Several following coaches were derailed.

Casualties: Four passengers were killed and one was fatally injured. Nineteen were detained in hospital with serious injuries.

Track: 95lb bull-head rail in 60ft lengths on wooden sleepers, laid in 1929. This section of track had been proposed for renewal in the 1948 programme.

Possible safety measures: The postwar shortage of materials and manpower made it difficult to maintain tracks to the required standard. There was a special need to impose speed restrictions where necessary.

Below: **POLESWORTH 21 July 1947**
The streamlined engine of the down Liverpool express is being rerailed. The tender and the first two coaches are seen still lying on their sides. ***Duncan Claridge Collection/IAL***

POLESWORTH
5.30am Monday 19 November 1951

Location: Near the signalbox.

The 10.30pm sleeping car express from Glasgow to Euston became derailed when passing through a crossover from the fast line to the slow line.

Cause: The driver missed the distant signal at caution and failed to reduce speed to the permanent restriction of 15mph. The train entered the crossover at about 55mph.

Conditions: Dark and clear.

Formation: 'Princess Coronation' class 4-6-2 No 46252 *City of Leicester* and 12 bogie vehicles, including six sleeping cars. There were 174 passengers.

Damage: The engine struck the up slow line platform and overturned. Eight coaches were derailed.

Casualties: Two passengers were injured.

Signalling: Absolute block with semaphore signalling and colour-light distants.

Possible safety measures: AWS at the distant signal would most probably have prevented this accident. It should be noted that the replacement of the semaphore distant signal by a colour-light signal was not effective in this case.

LICHFIELD
6.58pm Tuesday 1 January 1946

Location: Lichfield No 1 signalbox, at the crossover from the up fast line to the up slow line just beyond the north end of the platform.

The 6.8pm passenger train from Stafford to Nuneaton was diverted to the up slow line through the crossover at No 1 signalbox, in order to reach the platform (there were no platforms on the fast lines).

The signalman replaced the crossover points lever and then pulled off all his signal levers for the 2.50pm fish train from Fleetwood to London Broad Street to overtake the passenger train along the up fast line. However, the crossover points had not moved, and the fish train was diverted through them from the fast line and into the rear of the stationary passenger train at 35mph.

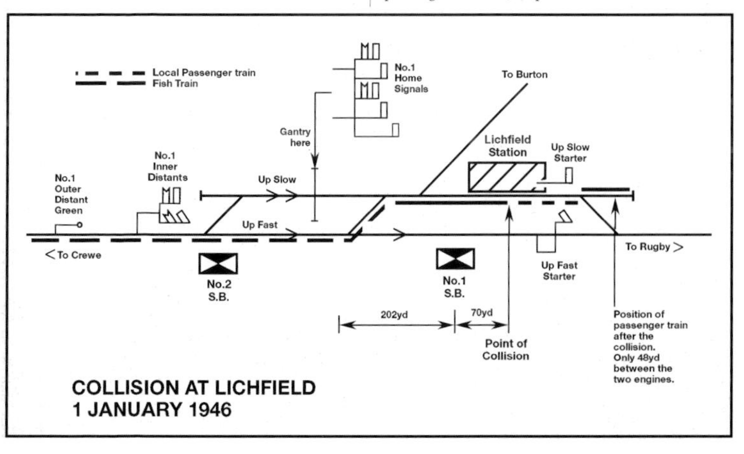

COLLISION AT LICHFIELD
1 JANUARY 1946

Cause: Some frozen ballast impeded the movement of the rocking bar at the crossover facing points, with the result that the bolt was not completely withdrawn, and the points remained in the reverse position when the signalman moved the point lever. He was able to move the point lever to its full stroke because the operating rod which ran for 200yd from the signalbox to the points buckled under his pressure. It was insufficiently guided. He also managed to move the home signal lever to its full stroke, although the signal arm did not respond, being held by the detection apparatus which ensured that the indication of the junction signal arms corresponded with the direction in which the points were set. The fact that the signalman was able to move all his stop signal levers to their required position for the fish train freed the interlocking and allowed the signalman to clear the distant signal. The signalman did not check the backlight of the home signal to ensure that it obeyed the lever.

Conditions: Dark and frosty.

Formations: *The passenger train* — ex-LNW 'Prince of Wales' class 4-6-0 No 25802 and four wooden-bodied non-corridor bogie coaches.
The fish train — Class 5P 4-6-0 No 5495 and seven four-wheeled fishvans.

Damage: Rear three coaches were totally destroyed and the fourth one was seriously damaged.

Casualties: 20 passengers lost their lives and 21 were injured.

Signalling: Absolute block with semaphore signalling and a colour-light outer distant signal.

Possible safety measures: More guidance rollers to prevent buckling of the point rod. Detection of the home signal arm, rather than the lever, to control the interlocking.

COLWICH
2.17pm Saturday 28 October 1911

Location: Down main line, in the station.

The 1.8pm stopping passenger train from Walsall to Stoke-on-Trent approached Colwich on the down slow line, but failed to stop at the home signal and went out on to the down main line before coming to a stand at the south end of the station. The signalman had already cleared his down line signals for an American boat train special from Euston to Liverpool, and although he put them back to danger when he saw what had happened, the boat train had already passed the distant signal in the clear position. Its driver saw the home signal at danger 500yd away and reduced speed, but was unable to avoid a collision, which took place at about 20mph.

Cause: The driver of the stopping passenger train passed a signal at danger, and the signalman should not have accepted the express until he was sure that the local train had come to a stand at his home signal.

Formations: *1.8pm Walsall to Stoke* — tank engine and six vehicles.
The boat train — double-headed, with an 'Experiment' class 4-6-0 and a 'Precursor' class 4-4-0, hauling 12 bogie corridor vehicles including five 12-wheelers.

Damage: *The local train* — the last two coaches were badly smashed.
The boat train — the pilot engine was damaged, but there was little damage to the train.

Casualties: Two with severe injuries.

Signalling: Absolute block with semaphore signals.

Possible safety measures: Strict adherence by signalmen to the block regulations regarding junction acceptance. There were no facing trap points at the end of the down slow line.

COLWICH
6.28pm Friday 19 September 1986

Location: Diamond crossing of the junction where the down Manchester line crosses the up main line.

The 17.00 express passenger train from Euston to Manchester Piccadilly, which had just been diverted from the down fast line to the down slow line to await a passage over the junction to the Manchester line, failed to stop at the junction signal at danger and came to a stand with the locomotive on the diamond crossing. The 17.20 express passenger train from Liverpool Lime Street to Euston was closely approaching the junction on the up main line, running at 95-100mph under clear signals, and its driver had no time to reduce speed, colliding almost immediately with the Manchester locomotive.

Cause: The driver of the Manchester train failed to stop at the junction signal at danger. He had misunderstood a new system of 'flashing yellow' junction signalling applied to the turnout from the down fast line to the down slow line.

Formations: *The Manchester train* — electric locomotive No 86429 with 12 coaches and a bogie brakevan. It conveyed 373 passengers.
The Liverpool train — electric locomotive No 86211 with a bogie brakevan and 11 coaches. It conveyed about 500 passengers.

Damage: *The Manchester train* — the locomotive and first two coaches were thrown on to their sides and damaged beyond repair. The next two coaches were extensively damaged.
The Liverpool train — the locomotive and first five vehicles were damaged beyond repair. The locomotive and one coach turned over on to their sides, whilst three of the others slewed across the tracks and came to rest on top of the second coach of the Manchester train.

Casualties: The driver of the Liverpool train was fatally injured, and 32 seriously injured passengers were detained in hospital.

Signalling: Track circuit block, with multiple-aspect colour-light signalling and continuous track circuiting. AWS was provided at all signals, which were controlled by Colwich signalbox, adjacent to the site of the accident.

Possible safety measures: Automatic train protection, checking that the driver of the Manchester train was braking correctly, would have prevented this accident. Better supervision and training of drivers might also have done so.

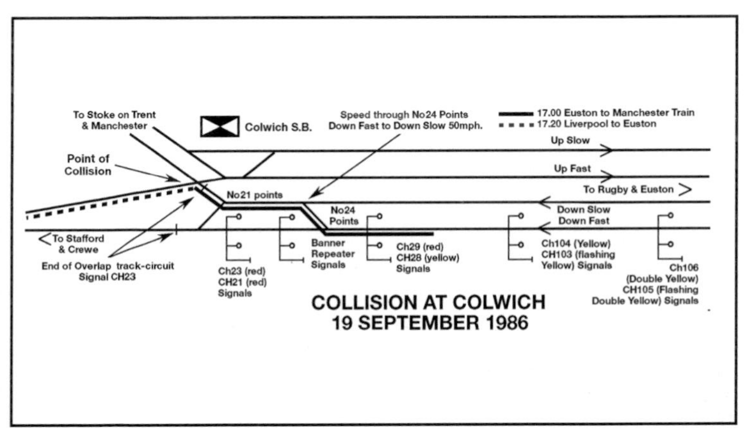

Above: **COLWICH 19 September 1986**
Colwich Junction looking north. The collision occurred on the diamond crossing in the centre of the photograph where the group of workmen can be seen. *Author*

STAFFORD
7.16pm Saturday 7 December 1946

Location: Down fast line just south of Stafford No 4 signalbox.

The 4.35pm stopping passenger train from Coventry to Stafford was standing on the down fast line with the engine opposite Stafford No 4 signalbox, when it was run into in the rear by the 3.45pm express passenger train from Euston to Liverpool Lime Street.

Cause: Signalman's error. He accepted the Liverpool express before the stopping train had passed through the section.

Formations: *The stopping train* — 2-6-4 tank engine No 2487 with four bogie vehicles. Lightly loaded with passengers.
The Liverpool express — 'Patriot' class 4-6-0 No 5500 *Patriot* (pilot engine) and 'Patriot' class 4-6-0 No 5512 *Bunsen* (train engine) with 13 bogie vehicles.

Damage: The rear coach of the local train was telescoped by the express engine, and there was also telescoping between the second and third coaches. The express train was virtually undamaged.

Casualties: One passenger died in hospital and one was injured.

Signalling: Absolute block with semaphore signals.

Possible safety measures: Track circuiting and the associated controls would have prevented this accident.

STAFFORD
12.30am Saturday 4 August 1990

Location: Up slow line at No 4 platform, Stafford station.

The 22.18 express passenger train from Manchester Piccadilly to Penzance was standing at No 4 platform when it was run into in the rear by an empty stock train which had been correctly signalled into the same platform under a special caution.

Cause: The empty stock train had been signalled into the platform under the authority of a position-light signal which indicated to the driver that the line ahead was occupied by another train, but he failed to regulate the speed of his train properly and was unable to stop before colliding with the rear of the Penzance train at about 20mph.

Conditions: Clear.

Formations: *The Penzance train* — diesel-electric locomotive No 47841 with nine coaches.
The empty stock train — Class 310 four-car electric multiple-unit.

Damage: *The Penzance train* — minor, except to the last coach, a corridor brake first.
The empty stock train — minor, except to the first coach, a driving trailer open.

Casualties: The driver of the empty stock train was killed when his driving cab was crushed. There were no serious injuries to passengers.

Signalling: Track circuit block with multiple-aspect colour-light signalling and continuous track circuiting. The signal concerned was a four-aspect colour-light signal No SD5 139, with junction route indicator and position light signal. The signalling in the area was controlled from Stafford No 5 signalbox. AWS was provided.

Possible safety measures: The driver had worked on 26 consecutive days before the accident, with a substantial amount of overtime, and had been drinking, but whether this contributed to the accident cannot be proved. In case it did, stricter controls were imposed on working hours and drinking.

GREAT BRIDGEFORD
7.52pm Friday 17 June 1932

Location: Up slow line to up fast line crossover, almost immediately south of Great Bridgeford station.

The 7.23pm passenger train from Crewe to Birmingham New Street was being diverted from the up slow line to the up fast line through a 15mph crossover, as a normal regulating function, but the train entered the crossover at not less than 50mph and was derailed.

Cause: In subsequent investigation it was not possible to resolve a conflict between the evidence of the driver and that of the signalman as to whether the distant signal was in the clear position or not. Did the driver fail to observe the distant signal in the caution position; or was it clear when he passed it but was then subsequently replaced to caution when the signalman decided to divert the train across to the fast line and reversed his junction facing points?

Formation: Ex-LNW rebuilt 'Precursor' class 4-4-0 No 5278 *Precursor* and four coaches. There were about 80 passengers in the train.

Damage: The engine turned over on to its side and the first coach was wrecked, being thrown across all four lines. The body of the second coach was demolished for two-thirds of its length.

Casualties: Four passengers lost their lives. The two enginemen and nine passengers were detained in hospital.

Signalling: Absolute block with semaphore signals. The distant signal was a semaphore. The section signals were free from block control — they did not need a 'Line Clear' release.

Possible safety measures: If the distant signal was passed in the caution position, and if AWS had been provided, it would probably have prevented the accident.

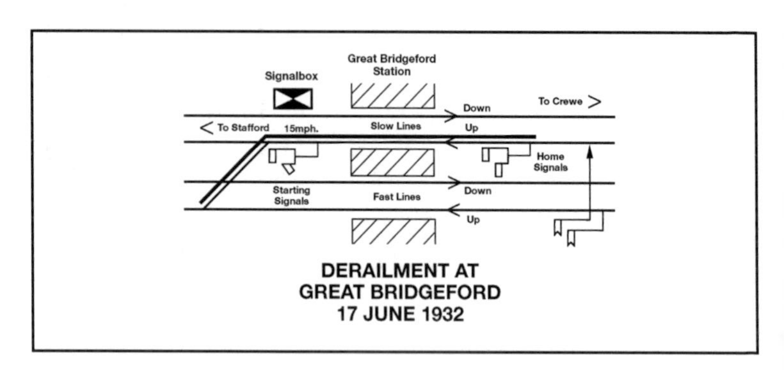

BETLEY ROAD
6.34am Wednesday 17 November 1954

Location: Between Wrine Hill and Betley Road signalboxes, about ¼-mile south of Betley Road station. The two signalboxes were approximately a mile apart.

The 12.45am Class D freight train from Camden to Carlisle, running on the down slow line at about 35mph, ran into the back of the 3am Class E freight train from Nuneaton to Crewe, which was just beginning to move away from the home signal at Betley Road signalbox.

Cause: The driver of the Carlisle freight train passed at danger the home signal of the previous signalbox,

Wrine Hill, and continued into the section ahead.

Conditions: Cold and dark, with a thick fog. Visibility 20yd.

Formations: *The Carlisle train* — 'Patriot' class 4-6-0 No 45546 *Fleetwood*, 25 wagons and brakevan.
The Crewe train — double-headed with 58 wagons and brakevan.

Damage: The engine of the Carlisle train, No 45546, turned over on to its side. The brakevan and several wagons of the Crewe train were derailed and damaged.

Casualties: The driver of the Carlisle train was fatally injured. The fireman and guard of the Crewe train were injured and taken to hospital.

Signalling: Absolute block. The home signal on the down slow line at Wrine Hill signalbox was a three-aspect colour-light signal, and also acted as Betley Road signalbox's distant signal. The down slow line distant signal for Wrine Hill was also a colour-light signal. Fog signalmen were not employed at colour-light signals.

Possible safety measures: AWS at Wrine Hill distant would most probably have prevented this accident.

Above: **BETLEY ROAD 17 November 1954**
The 'Patriot' class engine of the down Carlisle freight train is seen lying on its side. ***K. Roberts/IAL***

CREWE COAL YARD SIGNALBOX
4.25am Tuesday 16 November 1937

Location: 383yd north of Crewe Coal Yard signalbox. Approx ¾-mile north of Crewe North Junction.

The 10.30pm sleeping car express from Glasgow to Euston had just restarted from the up fast line home signal at Coal Yard signalbox, when it was run into at the rear, at about 15mph, by the 8.30pm sleeping car express from Perth to Euston.

Cause: The Perth train ran at low speed past all the signals at danger at the previous signalbox, Coppenhall Junction, and continued for 1½ miles through the block section. The signalman at

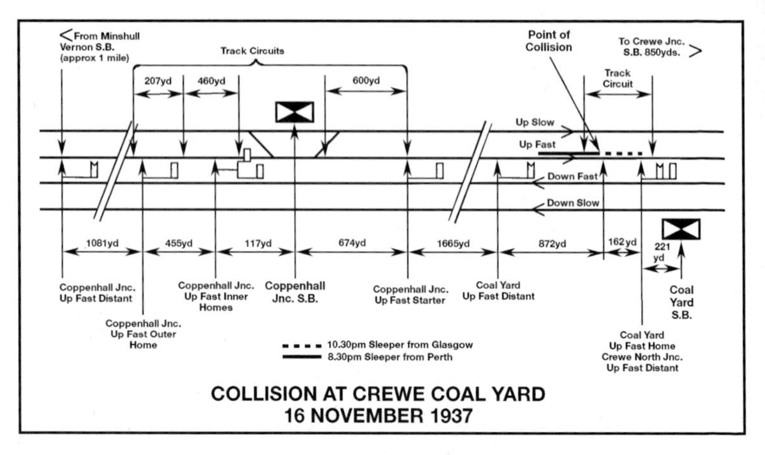

COLLISION AT CREWE COAL YARD
16 NOVEMBER 1937

Coppenhall Junction held both arms above his head as an indication to the driver to stop, but the driver thought it was an indication that the starting signal was off. The emergency detonator at the signalbox was exploded, but was not heard by the locomen.

Conditions: Darkness and dense fog. Fog signalmen were on duty.

Formations: *The Glasgow sleeper* — 'Royal Scot' class engine, bogie brakevan, four sleeping cars, and a bogie brakevan.
The Perth sleeper — 'Royal Scot' class engine, horsebox, bogie brakevan, five coaches (including three sleepers), two bogie brakevans and two fishvans.

Damage: *The Glasgow sleeper* — substantial damage, but not to the bodywork.
The Perth sleeper — some damage to engine and first two vehicles.

Casualties: The Glasgow guard was badly injured. There were several minor injuries.

Signalling: Absolute block, with semaphore signalling, including the distant signals.

Possible safety measures: A single-shot detonator placing machine had already been installed in Coppenhall Junction signalbox, and it was operated by the signalman when he realised that the train was running past his signals. However, the enginemen stated that they did not hear the explosion. Subsequently, detonator placing machines were equipped with two detonators to increase the noise of the explosion. AWS would not have prevented this accident, because the driver knew that the distant signal was at caution and he had reduced the speed of his train.

BETWEEN WINSFORD STATION AND COPPENHALL JUNCTION SIGNALBOXES
6.1pm Boxing Day, Wednesday 26 December 1962

Location: Up fast line near Milepost 164, approx 1½ miles south of Winsford station.

The 4.45pm express passenger train from Liverpool Lime Street to Birmingham had been standing at automatic signal CJ110, which was showing a red aspect. The signal had just changed to yellow, and the driver had released the brakes and was just about to restart his train when it was run into in the rear, at about 20-25mph, by the 1.30pm 'Midday Scot' from Glasgow to Euston.

Above: **BETWEEN WINSFORD STATION AND COPPENHALL JUNCTION SIGNALBOXES 26 December 1962**
Holbeck shed's 'Royal Scot' class 4-6-0 No 46108 *Seaforth Highlander* on a down Workington express at Minshull Vernon on 26 May 1958, about a mile south of the site of the collision. The signalling was modernised in the intervening four years and Minshull Vernon signalbox was closed. *T. Lewis/IAL*

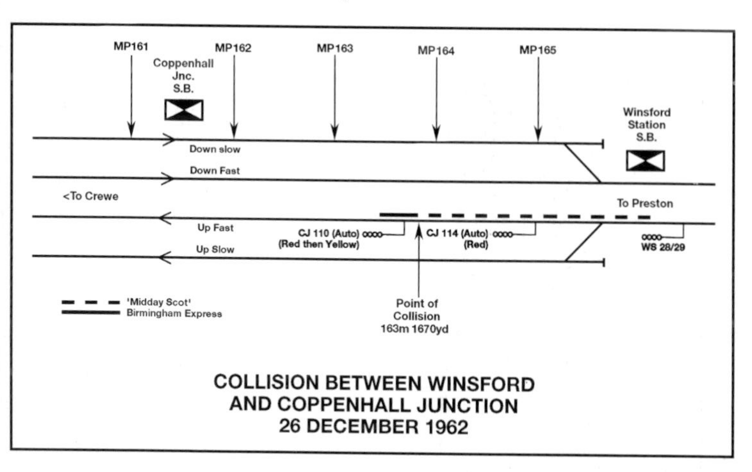

Cause: The 'Midday Scot' was brought to a stand at automatic signal CJ114 in rear of the Birmingham train, but when the driver attempted to contact the signalman at Coppenhall Junction he was unable to do so because the telephones were out of order. After a short delay the driver proceeded past the signal at danger, but he allowed his train to gather too much speed. The driver should not have passed the signal without attempting to contact the signalman on another telephone, or until he had ascertained that the line was clear as far as the next signal. He did not see the Liverpool train until the last moment.

Conditions: Dark and frosty, but clear.

Formations: *The Birmingham train* — an electric locomotive and eight coaches. The train conveyed about 300 passengers.
The 'Midday Scot' — Class 4 diesel-electric locomotive and 13 coaches. The train conveyed about 500 passengers.

Damage: *The Birmingham train* — the last coach telescoped into the next one for half its length. *The 'Midday Scot'* — there was little damage.

Casualties: 18 passengers were killed and 33, plus the guard of the Birmingham train, were seriously injured. They were all travelling in the last two coaches of the Birmingham train.

Signalling: Multiple-aspect colour-light signals with continuous track-circuiting and AWS. The signals at the two signalboxes were controlled by the signalmen, but in the section there were several sets of signals worked automatically by the passage of trains. There were telephones to a signalbox at all signals.

Possible safety measures: Strict adherence to the appropriate rule, and tail lamps showing a brighter light.

WINSFORD
12.27am Saturday 17 April 1948

Location: Near Winsford Goods Yard signalbox (which was closed at the time), between the Junction and Station signalboxes.

The 5.40pm express passenger train from Glasgow to Euston was brought to a stand in mid-section when the communication cord was irregularly pulled. The driver had already released the brakes, when the following train, the 6.25pm Postal from Glasgow to Euston, was wrongly allowed to enter the section and ran into the back of the passenger train at 40-45mph.

Cause: The signalman at Winsford station signalbox wrongly assumed that the passenger train had passed his signalbox, even though he had not seen it, and he therefore accepted the following train, the Postal, allowing it to enter the section at full speed under clear signals.

Conditions: Dark but clear.

Formations: *The express* — 'Princess Royal' class Pacific No 6207 *Princess Arthur of Connaught* and 10 bogie vehicles.
The Postal — 'Princess Coronation' class Pacific No 6251 *City of Nottingham* and 13 bogie vans.

Damage: The last coach of the passenger train was demolished. Severe telescoping of the Postal took place. Many coaches and vans were derailed.

Casualties: 16 passengers were killed and eight were fatally injured, all in the last two coaches of the passenger train.

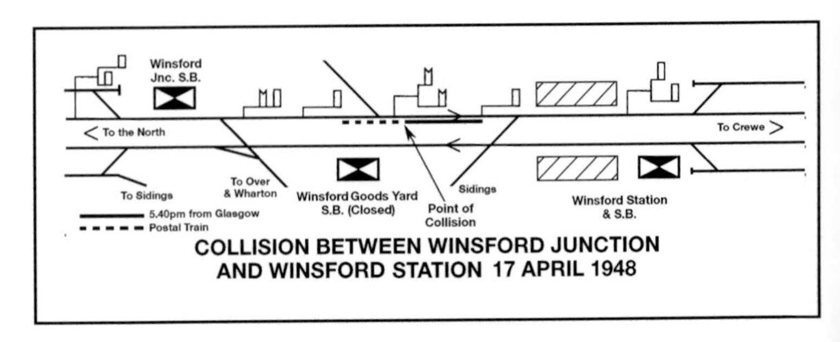

COLLISION BETWEEN WINSFORD JUNCTION AND WINSFORD STATION 17 APRIL 1948

Signalling: Absolute block, with semaphore signals.

Possible safety measures: Signalling equipment already existed to guard against a signalman assuming that a train had passed his signalbox when it had not done so, eg 'Sykes Lock and Block', widely installed on the Southern Railway, the Midland Railway's Rotary Block, and 'Welwyn Control', devised after a collision there in 1935. No such equipment had been installed on former LNWR lines. The traincrew of the passenger train were slow in protecting their train in the rear; had they done so promptly the collision may have been avoided, or at least its effects reduced.

WEAVER JUNCTION
10.12pm Wednesday 6 August 1975

Location: At the trailing junction between the up Liverpool line and the up Warrington line, at 174 miles 600yd.

A freightliner train, No 4068, the 18.05 from Coatbridge to Southampton, was running on the up Warrington line at 70-75mph under clear signals when another freight train, No 6F52, the 21.30 company train from Runcorn to Wallerscote, collided sideways on to it.

Cause: Train 6F52 ran past the junction-protecting signal at danger because it did not have sufficient braking capacity on the falling gradient of 1 in 101/151 for two miles approaching the junction signal. The train should have been reclassified to run at a lower speed but the marshalling yard staff at the starting point of the train, and the guard, failed to do so. The driver should also have braked more severely on the falling gradient.

Conditions: Fine.

Formations: *The freightliner train* — electric locomotive No 86103 and 15 freightliner vehicles, some loaded.

The company train — diesel-electric locomotive No 40189 and 20 45-ton tanks loaded with caustic soda.

Damage: The last 10 freightliner vehicles were derailed and damaged. The diesel locomotive was derailed and damaged. It came to rest leaning on its side. The first 15 tank wagons were derailed, and several were pierced, allowing about 250 tons of caustic soda liquor to be spilled out.

Casualties: None serious.

Signalling: Track circuit block, and multiple-aspect colour-light signalling with continuous track circuiting and AWS, controlled from Weaver Junction signalbox.

Possible safety measures: Better training in the calculation of brake forces in relation to allowable train speeds. Better supervision of train preparation staff. The calculations were complex, and some tank wagons had air brakes, some had vacuum brakes.

BETWEEN NORTON CROSSING AND ACTON GRANGE JUNCTION
2.45am Friday 15 September 1957

Location: Moore water troughs, about midway between the two signalboxes.

The 11.55pm sleeping car express from Euston to Barrow-in-Furness became derailed as it travelled at about 75mph over Moore water troughs.

Cause: A pair of fishplates holding in line two lengths of rail became detached and fell away, owing to the nuts securing the fishplates firmly against the rails running off the bolts which ran through holes in the rail-ends and the fishplates. This allowed the rail-ends to move out of line.

Above: **WEAVER JUNCTION 6 August 1975**
An aerial view of the wreckage of the two trains, looking south. There appears to be remarkably little activity.
Author's collection

Formation: Type 4 English Electric diesel-electric locomotive, bogie brakevan, four passenger coaches, five sleeping cars, bogie brakevan. The train conveyed 53 passengers.

Damage: The train became derailed, but all the coaches stayed upright and in line.

Casualties: Negligible.

Track: 97½lb 60ft bullhead rails laid new in 1961 in cast iron chairs with teak keys, on new sleepers.

Possible safety measures: Improved specification of nuts and bolts, and improved track inspection procedures.

NEAR ACTON GRANGE JUNCTION SIGNALBOX
11.58pm Friday 13 May 1966

Location: About ½-mile south of Acton Grange Junction signalbox, between Mileposts 179½ and 179¾, on the down main line.

The line between Norton Crossing and Acton Grange Junction signalboxes lies in a hollow, the last mile being on a rising gradient of 1 in 135. A freight train, the 23.00 Class 8 from Northwich to St Helens, had become divided in running on the falling gradient, but momentum had kept the second portion running for a time when it came on to the rising gradient and passed Acton Grange Junction signalbox. The signalman did not notice that the train was divided, and sent the 'Train out of Section' signal to Norton Crossing signalbox. He was then offered and accepted the 20.40 sleeping car express from Euston to Stranraer, which had already entered the section when he noticed the rear portion of the freight train coming back towards him and running away in the wrong direction. The guard was unable to control it and it continued to run back until it collided with the locomotive of the Stranraer express. The signalman decided not to divert the runaway wagons through his crossover to the right line.

Both movements took place at fairly low speed; the express was moving quite slowly because it had passed the distant signal in the caution position, and the guard estimated its speed to be about 25mph when the collision took place.

Cause: The coupling of the second wagon jumped off the hook of the third wagon during the journey. It was a screw coupling and had not been tightened; it was completely unscrewed.

Formations: *The Stranraer express* — Class 4 English Electric diesel-electric locomotive No D322 and 10 coaches, including two sleepers.
The freight train — Class 8F 2-8-0 steam engine and 31 loaded wagons and brakevan.

Damage: The cab of the Stranraer locomotive was crushed, but the train was not seriously damaged. Thirteen freight wagons and the brakevan were derailed and several were severely damaged.

Casualties: The driver and secondman of the Stranraer express were killed.

Signalling: Absolute block with semaphore signals and colour-light distants. There were catch points in the section to derail runaway wagons, but the express had already passed them when the collision occurred.

Possible safety measures: Abolish loose-coupled freight trains. In the meantime, the signalmen at Acton Grange Junction were instructed not to give the 'Train out of Section' signal to Norton Crossing signalbox for a loose-coupled train until it had passed completely clear of the rising gradient, just over ¼-mile beyond the signalbox.

WINWICK JUNCTION (WARRINGTON)
9.10pm Friday 28 September 1934

Location: 40yd south of the down home signals at Winwick Junction signalbox.

The 8.55pm local train from Warrington to Wigan was moving forward slowly from the down home signal at Winwick Junction signalbox, after having been brought to a stand there, when it was run into violently in the rear by the 5.20pm express passenger train from Euston to Blackpool, travelling at about 50mph.

Cause: The signalman at Winwick Junction had overlooked the presence of the local train standing at his signals. He noticed the block indicator for that section showing 'Train on Line' and jumped to the conclusion that he must have forgotten to give the 'Train out of Section' signal to the signalbox in rear (Winwick Quay) for the previous train, whereas in reality it was showing 'Train on Line' for the local train. He therefore sent 'Train out of Section' at once and moved his block indicator to the normal position. He was immediately offered the express, which he accepted and cleared all his signals for. The driver of the local train saw the down home signal move to the clear position and he was drawing forward slowly to pick up his fireman (who was walking to the signalbox 200yd away to remind the signalman of the presence of his train at the down home signal), when the collision occurred. Unfortunately, the fireman did not have time to reach the signalbox.

Conditions: Fine and dark.

Formations: *The local train* — ex-LNW 2-4-2T No 6632 and three bogie coaches.
The express — ex-LNW 'Prince of Wales' class 4-6-0 No 25648 and nine bogie coaches.

Damage: *The local train* — the second coach was badly damaged and the third was completely destroyed.
The express — the first two coaches were telescoped and wrecked.

Casualties: Five passengers and the guard of the local train, and three passengers in the express, were killed. Two more died in hospital. Eighteen passengers and the driver of the local train were injured and taken to hospital.

Signalling: Absolute block with semaphore signalling.

Possible safety measures: Electrical controls on the signalling equipment to prevent the signalman from accepting a train until the previous train has been proved to have passed through the rear section. Several companies had installed such equipment, eg 'Sykes Lock and Block' on the Southern and other companies, and Rotary Block on the Midland. A track circuit at the home signal could have performed a similar function by holding the block indicator at 'Train on Line'.

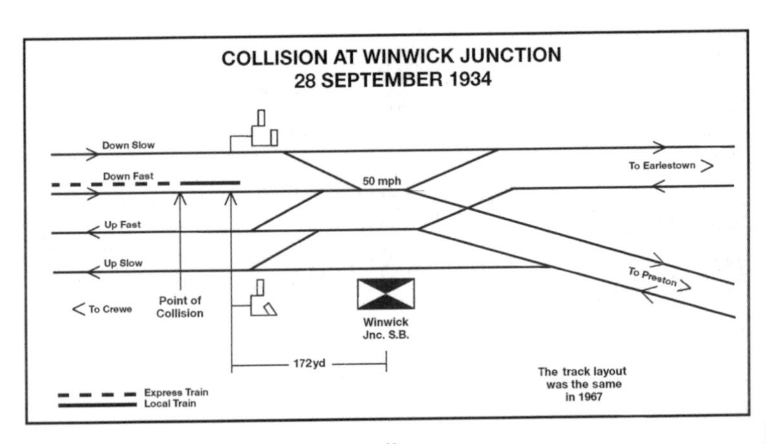

WINWICK JUNCTION (WARRINGTON)
10.50am Tuesday 11 July 1967

Location: 360yd south of Winwick Junction signalbox down home signals.

A Class 5 freight train was standing at Winwick Junction down fast line home signal, and was just about to move off when it was run into at the rear, at a speed of about 20mph, by the 10.11 two-car diesel multiple-unit (DMU) from Chester to Manchester Exchange. The DMU was slowing down because Winwick Junction's distant was in the caution position and the driver noticed that the home signals were cleared for the wrong direction; he was therefore preparing to stop at the signalbox to query the route.

Cause: The driver of the DMU had mistakenly read the down home signal at the previous signalbox, Winwick Quay, as being in the clear position, although the signal lever was back in the frame and the signal was intended to be in the danger position. The arm was standing at about 17° above horizontal, in a position known as 'halfcock'. The signal equipment had not been properly maintained and supervision was inadequate. The signalman had omitted to satisfy himself, when he last replaced the lever in the frame, that the signal arm actually obeyed the lever and moved to the horizontal position.

Conditions: Fine and sunny.

Formations: *The passenger train* — a two-car DMU.
The freight train — a Class 5 4-6-0 steam engine No 45061 with 37 wagons and a brakevan.

Damage: Fairly minor damage to the DMU. Several wagons of the freight train were derailed.

Casualties: One person was detained in hospital.

Signalling: Absolute block with semaphore signals and colour-light distants. AWS was provided.

Possible safety measures: Better maintenance of signalling equipment and supervision of staff. Drivers not to accept a 'halfcock' signal as intended to be in the clear position. Signalmen to be more vigilant when replacing signal levers.

Above: **WINWICK JUNCTION 28 September 1934 and 11 July 1967**
'Britannia' class Pacific No 70028 *Royal Star* takes the up slow line at Winwick Junction with an up West Coast main line parcels train on 1 April 1967. The line to Earlestown diverges to the left. View looking north.
J. S. Hancock/IAL

WIGAN NORTH WESTERN
3.55am Wednesday 20 December 1916

Location: North end of the station.

The 10pm passenger train from Euston had arrived at the down fast platform and was then drawn forward past No 4 signalbox in order to be backed into No 5 bay platform. Whilst the setting back movement was being performed, it was run into head-on by the 11.15pm sleeping car express from Euston to Edinburgh, which was travelling at 45-50mph.

Cause: The driver of the express had run past all the signals at danger at Wigan Nos 2 and 4 signalboxes. The signalman at No 1 signalbox had wrongly lowered his signals too soon for a non-stopping express which did not have a clear run through the station, possibly misleading the enginemen.

Formation: The Edinburgh train — pilot engine 2-4-0 No 604 *Narcissus* and train engine 'Prince of Wales' class 4-6-0 No 1324 *Falaba*, with 14 vehicles, marshalled three Post Office vans, coach, brakevan, nine coaches including three sleeping cars.

Damage: *The shunt movement* — the rear three vehicles were smashed-up and derailed.
The express — both engines were derailed and the pilot engine was badly damaged. The first five vehicles were derailed, the first four being damaged beyond repair.

Casualties: A guard and a Post Office sorter were killed and several people were injured.

Signalling: Absolute block with semaphore signals.

Possible safety measures: (1) A form of automatic train control. Before the war, several companies had been holding trials of different devices. (2) Signalmen must not lower the home signal too soon when the line ahead is not clear.

RIBBLE SIDINGS (PRESTON)
10.42pm Bank Holiday Monday 4 August 1930

Location: Near Ribble Sidings up slow starting signal.

A return excursion from Blackpool Central to Leeds was drawing forward slowly from the up slow starting signal when it was run into in the rear at low speed by another return excursion, from Blackpool Talbot Road to Birmingham.

Cause: The signalman had forgotten that the Leeds train was standing at his starting signal.

Conditions: Dark, but fine and clear.

Formations: *The Leeds train* — ex-LNW 'Prince of Wales' class 4-6-0 No 5803 and 11 bogie coaches.
The Birmingham train — Standard LMS 2-6-0 No 13036 and 12 bogie coaches.

Damage: Neither train suffered derailment or serious damage.

Casualties: One passenger was badly injured and 12 were slightly injured.

Signalling: Absolute block with semaphore signals. The signalbox in rear was Preston No 1. Ribble Sidings signalbox had an illuminated diagram, but there was no track circuit at the up slow starting signal.

Possible safety measures: Provision of a track circuit at the up slow starting signal.

SOUTH OF PRESTON STATION
6.45pm Saturday 18 January 1986

Location: Down fast line at signal PN76.

A football supporters' charter special train, returning from Carlisle to Accrington, failed to stop at Preston station, passed three signals at danger and finally collided at about 45mph with a stationary diesel-electric locomotive.

Cause: The train, a two-car diesel multiple-unit (DMU), failed to respond to a brake application by the driver. There was insufficient vacuum in the braking system of the train, because the vacuum had gradually been lost during the nonstop journey from Carlisle by inadvertent incorrect movement of the brake handle by the driver. It is likely that he was distracted by unauthorised passengers in the driving cab.

Conditions: Dark, windy and raining.

Formation: Two-car diesel multiple-unit. There were 115 passengers in the train.

Damage: The front cab of the diesel locomotive was destroyed. The front cab and the passenger compartment of the DMU were destroyed.

Casualties: 44 passengers were injured and taken to hospital, of whom four were detained.

Possible safety measures: Unauthorised persons not to travel in the driving cab.

HEST BANK
12 midnight Monday 22 July 1912

Location: Just south of the station.

The double-headed 8.50pm goods train from Manchester to Carlisle, conveying 49 wagons, had stopped at Hest Bank and, on restarting, the train had broken in two and left behind 14 empty wagons and a brakevan. A following train, the 11.28pm express passenger train from Preston to Carlisle, was wrongly allowed to approach and collided with the stationary rear portion of the goods train. The driver of the express saw the tail and side lights of the goods train and had braked to about 25mph when the collision occurred.

Cause: The enginemen of the goods train failed to look back when starting to check that the whole train was following. The goods guard went forward to the signalbox instead of going back along the line to protect his train. The signalman failed to notice the absence of tail and side lights when the goods train passed his signalbox, and irregularly accepted the express from the signalbox in rear.

Conditions: Clear.

Formation: The express — 'Experiment' class 4-6-0 No 1603 and six vehicles.

Damage: *The express* — only minor damage. *The goods train* — the brakevan and the last five wagons were derailed, with some damage.

Casualties: No serious injuries.

Possible safety measures: More careful adherence to rules and regulations by signalmen and traincrews.

HEST BANK
2.20am Thursday 20 May 1965

Location: At the water troughs, just north of the station.

The 22.10 sleeping car express from Glasgow to Kensington Olympia was derailed whilst travelling at about 70mph under clear signals.

Cause: A broken rail. A crack had developed from a

wheelburn and gradually extended along the rail, until a piece of rail 13ft long broke away as the third coach was passing over it.

Conditions: Clear, with ground frost.

Formation: Brush Type 4 diesel-electric locomotive, four coaches, seven sleeping cars and a bogie brakevan (12 vehicles). The train conveyed 114 passengers.

Damage: The locomotive and first three coaches were not derailed. The next four coaches came to rest on their sides between the platforms of Hest Bank station. The remainder came to rest tilted over on the side of a low embankment. There was considerable external damage, but little internal damage.

Casualties: Eleven passengers suffered minor injuries or shock, but only two were detained in hospital.

Possible safety measures: Prevent wheelspin. The removal of water troughs has eased the problem.

Above: **HEST BANK 22 July 1912 and 20 May 1965**
A southbound express from Barrow-in-Furness to Preston passes through Hest Bank station on 19 July 1958, double-headed by Class 5 4-6-0 No 44745 and 2-6-4T No 42317. ***F. Wilde/IAL***

BETWEEN OXENHOLME AND LAMBRIGG CROSSING 3.50pm Friday 10 September 1971

Location: At catch points in the down main line near the Milepost 22¼, about three miles north of Oxenholme.

Single line working was in operation between Lambrigg Crossing and Oxenholme using the down line, whilst the up line was being used for work in connection with the electrification of the West Coast main line. The 11.45 Motorail train from Stirling to Sutton Coldfield was travelling over the down line in the 'wrong' direction at about 15mph when it became derailed at some catch points.

Cause: The catch points, which had been fastened

in the closed position during the single line working, were wrongly released and allowed to open before single line working had finished, owing to a misunderstanding by one of the traffic inspectors on site. The driver of the Motorail train did not notice that there was no green flag at the catch points and when he noticed that they were open he was too close to prevent the derailment. He had approached the points at more than the stipulated 10mph.

Conditions: Fine and sunny.

Formation: Class 47 diesel-electric locomotive, six coaches (including two sleeping cars) and seven bogie carflats. There were 37 passengers in the train.

Damage: The engine and first three coaches (a passenger coach and two sleepers) ran down an embankment and turned on to their sides. The fourth and fifth coaches were also derailed. There was extensive external damage.

Casualties: No passengers were injured. They were travelling in the rear three coaches.

Possible safety measures: Strict adherence to the rules and regulations, and more care in passing verbal messages. Catch points were ultimately eliminated on this line when it was electrified, whereupon the remaining loose-coupled freight trains were diverted to the Settle and Carlisle route.

LAMBRIGG CROSSING
2.7pm Sunday 18 May 1947

Location: Near the signalbox (between Grayrigg and Oxenholme). The train stopped on Docker Viaduct.

Single line working was in operation over the down line in the section south of Lambrigg Crossing signalbox, owing to relaying operations taking place on the up line. It was therefore necessary for up trains to be set back to the down line through the crossover at Lambrigg Crossing, preparatory to passing over the down line in the wrong direction, but owing to the steep gradient an engine (Class 2P 4-4-0) was on-hand to assist up trains during the setting back movement. This engine stood on the up line well beyond both the crossover and the 440yd clearance point beyond the home signal. The 10am express passenger train from Glasgow to Euston

Above: **LAMBRIGG CROSSING 2.7pm Sunday 18 May 1947**
Class 5 4-6-0 No 44906 passes the signalbox at Lambrigg Crossing, scene of the accident two years previously.
W. Philip Connolly/IAL

approached Lambrigg Crossing at about 55mph and collided with the light engine at about 25/30mph.

Cause: The driver missed the distant signal, which was at caution, and observed the home signal at danger at short range. He braked, but was unable to stop his train before it collided with the light engine. The driver had approached the single line working too fast and was not paying proper attention.

Conditions: Drizzly, but visibility good.

Formation: 'Princess Coronation' class Pacific No 6235 *City of Birmingham* and 13 vehicles.

Damage: The express engine and the first three coaches were derailed but not seriously damaged, and one pair of wheels of the light engine's bogie was derailed.

Casualties: Three passengers and a dining car cook were injured and detained in hospital.

Possible safety measures: Automatic train control would have prevented this accident.

PENRITH
1.23am Saturday 5 December 1903

Location: 90yd north of the station.

The 8.10pm goods train from Liverpool to Carlisle became divided in running somewhere on the falling gradient from Shap, and this was noticed by the signalman at Eamont Junction. He sent a message 'Train Divided' to the signalman at Keswick Junction, 1,240yd to the north, who waved a green handsignal from side to side to the driver of the train. This handsignal warned the driver that his train had become divided and gave him authority to enter the next section, passing a signal at danger if necessary, in order to avoid stopping and risking the second portion of his train catching up and colliding with the first portion. However, the driver did stop, in Penrith station, with only two wagons attached, and the second portion, of 29 wagons, caught up and collided with the front portion, scattering some wagons foul of the up main line. An up sleeping car express, which had left Carlisle at 12.57am, ran into the wreckage at not less than 50mph.

Cause: Accidental uncoupling.

Formations: *The express* — four-coupled engine and six vehicles.
The goods train — four-cylinder compound goods engine, with 31 unbraked wagons and a brakevan.

Damage: All six vehicles of the express were derailed.

Casualties: The driver and fireman of the express were injured, but no passengers suffered injuries.

Possible safety measures: Trains frequently became divided in running in the days of loose-coupled goods trains, and it required great skill on the part of drivers and guards to avoid such an occurrence by avoiding snatches.

MOSSBAND
3.16am Monday 15 May 1944

Location: Approx 1¼ miles south of Gretna Junction.

The 8.40pm sleeping car express from Euston to Glasgow St Enoch, running under clear signals at about 55mph, became completely derailed except for the last two vehicles.

Cause: Unsatisfactory nature of subsoil below the permanent way, which had been undergoing extensive maintenance work the previous day.

Formation: 'Princess Coronation' class Pacific No 6225 *Duchess of Gloucester*, with 12 bogie vehicles, including five 12-wheeled sleepers.

Damage: The engine turned over at 45°, whilst the tender was turned on to its side. The whole train except the last two vehicles was derailed.

Casualties: Three passengers were killed.

Possible safety measures: Temporary speed restrictions should be imposed after such work.

GRETNA JUNCTION
6.9pm Tuesday 5 November 1940

Location: At the diamond of the junction, where the up line from the G&SW route from Dumfries crosses the down ex-Caledonian Railway line to Lockerbie.

The 8.55am goods train from Shawfield to Carlisle was crossing the junction off the G&SW route, when it was run into sideways-on at the tender and first few wagons by the 10.5am express passenger train from Euston to Perth, running under clear signals at about 45mph. The junction facing points in the down line were set towards Lockerbie.

Cause: There was a conflict of evidence that was not resolved. The signalman maintained that he had never cleared the signals for the goods train, which should therefore have stopped at his outer home signal until the Perth express had cleared the junction. On the other hand, the driver of the goods train said that the outer and inner distant signals were at caution, but that the outer home signal was clear. He then saw the inner home signal at danger too late to stop clear of the junction. The fireman said that when he first saw the inner distant it was at caution, but it was then cleared. The question that was not resolved was whether the signalman had originally set the junction and cleared his signals for the goods train and had then changed his mind when he realised that the express was near, and had put back to danger and caution the signals for the goods train and altered his junction and signals in favour of the express, or whether the signals had never been cleared for the goods train and the driver had passed them at danger.

Conditions: Raining heavily and almost dark.

Formations: *The Perth express* — Standard compound 4-4-0 No 1141 and 10 bogie vehicles. *The goods train* — ex-Caledonian 4-6-0 No 14650, 45 unbraked wagons and a brakevan.

Damage: The Perth express — the compound was turned over on to its side and the first five coaches were derailed.

Casualties: The driver of the compound and two passengers were killed, and 40 people were detained in hospital.

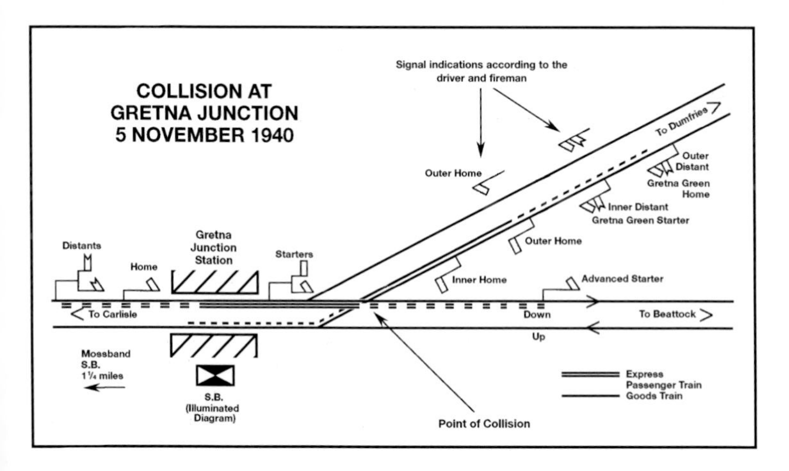

Above: **GRETNA JUNCTION 5 November 1940**
A Liverpool to Glasgow express takes the former Caledonian Railway main line at Gretna Junction on 9 September 1961, headed by 'Jubilee' class 4-6-0 No 45628 *Somaliland. D. Cross*

Signalling: Absolute block. The signals approaching the junction off the G&SW, and their distances from the point of collision, were: up outer distant 1,764yd, up inner distant 1,049yd, up outer home 531yd, up inner home 31yd.

Possible safety measures: Doubt about the indications of the distant signals coming off the G&SW would have been resolved by AWS, but if the signalman did put his signals back against the goods train after having given it clear signals he committed a very serious irregularity. Had the signalman allowed the goods train to have priority over the junction and had never cleared his signals for the Perth express, the facing points in the down line would have had to be set towards the G&SW to protect against an overrun. The interlocking would have required the points to be so set before the junction trailing points could be set for a movement off the G&SW. This is known as flank protection.

QUINTINSHILL
6.50am Saturday 22 May 1915

Location: 60yd from Quintinshill signalbox.

A troop train special from Larbert to Liverpool, running easily down the long falling gradient of 1 in 200 on the up main line at 60mph or more under clear signals, collided head-on, engine to engine, with a local passenger train which had been shunted through the crossover road from the down main line, to stand on the up main line out of the way of a down Scotch express. A few moments later the Scotch express, also travelling at full speed under clear signals, crashed into the wreckage. Fire then broke out and consumed much of the wreckage.

Cause: The signalman had forgotten that the local passenger train was standing on the up main line. He had therefore cleared all his signals for the troop train. The signalmen were changing shifts and both were involved. The troop train had been preceded by a goods train, which had been turned into the loop at Quintinshill, and when it was clear of the up main line the signalman had sent the 'Train out of Section'

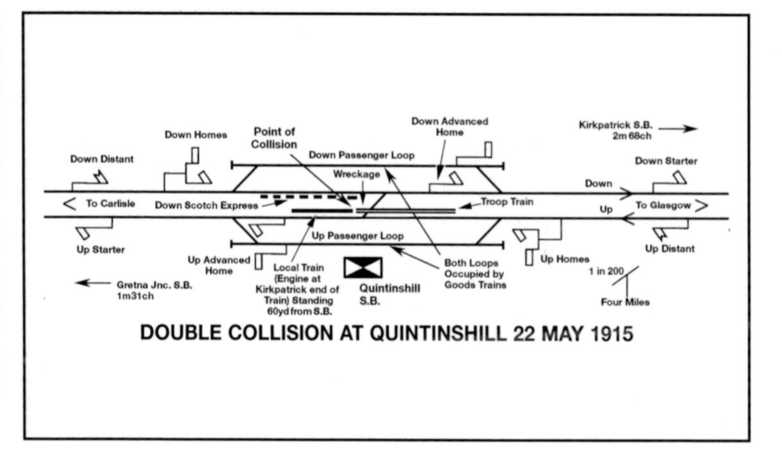

DOUBLE COLLISION AT QUINTINSHILL 22 MAY 1915

signal to the signalbox in rear, Kirkpatrick. He should then have maintained his block indicator at 'Train on Line' and sent the bell signal 'Blocking Back inside Home Signal' to protect the local train, but he failed to do so.

The fireman of the local train had gone to the signalbox as soon as his train had been crossed to the up line, in order to remind the signalman of its presence as required by rule. The fireman should then have remained in the signalbox as a continuing reminder, unless the signalman had confirmed that he had taken protective measures (ie blocking back, and placing a metal collar over the up main line home signal to prevent its being cleared in error). The signalman did not take any protective measures, and the fireman returned to his train without that vital assurance.

Formations: *The local train* (6.10am from Carlisle) — Caledonian Railway 4-6-0 No 907, three bogie coaches and a milk van.
The troop special — Caledonian Railway 4-4-0 No 121, 15 Great Central Railway six- and eight-wheeled coaches, mostly gaslit, and six trucks and vans of equipment.
The Scotch express (12 midnight Euston to Glasgow) — two Caledonian Railway 4-4-0s, Nos 140 (pilot) and 48 (train engine), and 13 bogie vehicles.

Damage: Very considerable. Virtually all 15 coaches of the troop train were destroyed and consumed by fire.

Casualties: *The local train* — two passengers were killed.
The troop train — 215 passengers were killed, together with the driver and fireman.
The Scotch express — seven passengers were killed.
In addition there were several hundred injured.
This was the most serious accident in the whole history of Britain's railways.

Signalling: Absolute block, with semaphore signals. There were no track circuits.

Possible safety measures: In 1915 signalling safety required signalmen and traincrews to perform their duties with meticulous observance of the rules and regulations. Track circuits on the up main line would have detected the presence of the local train and locked the up home signal at danger, but they were a relatively new device in 1915 and there were other locations in greater need.

Most of the coaches of the troop train had wooden underframes and would probably not have been used in a train of this nature in peacetime. The heap of wooden wreckage was ignited by live coals from the fireboxes of the various engines. It was to be many years before wooden coaches were completely withdrawn from service — they provided insufficient protection in an accident and they caught fire too easily.

QUINTINSHILL
Friday 12 January 1973

Location: Up main line in rear of the up main starting signal.

Freight train 8M48, the 03.48 from Dalzell New Yard to Carlisle, was standing at the starting signal at Quintinshill, when it was run into at the rear by freight train 8M45, the 04.12 from Mossend to Carlisle.

Cause: The driver of 8M45 admitted dozing off after seeing the up distant signal at caution, but he must have acknowledged the AWS warning as a reflex action. He then passed two stop signals at danger. The driver admitted taking alcohol immediately before signing on.

Formations: *8M48* — Class 37 diesel-electric locomotive No 6854.
8M45 — Class 37 diesel-electric locomotive No 6843.

Damage: 41 wagons were derailed and piled up, 32 being damaged beyond repair.

Casualties: The guard of train 8M48 was badly injured.

Possible safety measures: Stricter controls on the consumption of alcohol before taking duty. Automatic train protection (ATP) would have prevented this accident.

Above: **QUINTINSHILL 12 January 1973**
Breakdown cranes are working to clear the line of wrecked and derailed wagons. ***G. Kingborn/IAL***

BETWEEN ECCLEFECHAN AND KIRTLEBRIDGE
9.12pm Friday 6 April 1906

Location: Near Milepost 18, 1¼ miles south of Ecclefechan.

The 7pm express goods from Glasgow to London was running under clear signals at 50/55mph when the third wagon from the engine left the rails. The following wagons became derailed and fouled the down main line. The 8.42pm passenger train from Carlisle ran into the wreckage.

Cause: The breakage of a Mansell wheel on a West Coast Joint Stock refrigerated van.

Formations: *The express goods* — a 4-4-0 passenger engine and 17 fully-braked wagons.
The passenger train — a 4-4-0 passenger engine and 11 vehicles, equal to 17 in length.

Damage: The passenger train — the engine and tender, and first three coaches, overturned.

Casualties: One passenger was killed and 12 were injured.

Possible safety measures: No reason for the breakage of the wheel could be found. Mansell wheels (made partly of wood) were eventually phased out. The possibility of issuing the guards of trains with fusees (red flares) was again raised, but did not find favour. It was intended that they should be ignited when a train became disabled or suffered a mishap in mid-section, to alert and warn the driver of any approaching train. This question was reconsidered at intervals until as recently as the 1980s, but the provision of flares was never adopted by the railways.

ECCLEFECHAN
3.7pm Saturday 21 July 1945

Location: Trailing points with the refuge siding in the up main line.

The 1pm express passenger train from Glasgow to London passed the up distant signal at caution and the up outer and inner home signals at danger and collided sidelong at about 60-65mph with the fourth wagon of a goods train which was being set back off the up main line into the refuge siding to clear the line for the express.

Cause: The driver wrongly passed the signals at danger.

Conditions: Raining.

Formations: *The express* — 'Princess Coronation' class Pacific No 6231 *Duchess of Atholl*, a bogie brakevan, 11 coaches and a bogie brakevan.
The goods train — Standard Class 4F 0-6-0 No 4324, 45 wagons and brakevan.

Damage: The Pacific and the first vehicle were overturned, and several coaches were derailed but remained upright and in line.

Casualties: The driver and fireman of the Pacific were killed. A total of 31 injured passengers were taken to hospital.

Signalling: Absolute block with semaphore signals. A colour-light up distant signal had been planned prewar but had not yet been installed.

Possible safety measures: ATC/AWS was the only reliable safeguard in a case like this.

DINWOODIE
3am Thursday 25 October 1928

Location: Between Dinwoodie and Wamphray, approximately two miles south of Wamphray station.

The 7.30pm 'Royal Highlander' express passenger train, running under clear signals at over 60mph, ran into the rear of the 1.20am goods train from

Carlisle to Dundee which had failed in section with an engine defect.

Cause: The signalman at Wamphray accepted the goods train from Dinwoodie, and after it had entered the section he dozed off. A short while later he woke and, seeing his block indicator still at 'Train in Section' (for the goods train) he jumped to the conclusion that it must have passed whilst he was asleep, and gave 'Train out of Section' for it. He then accepted the express, which entered the section under clear signals. The goods train had been at a stand for about 15min and the guard was slow in protecting his train; he was only 300-400yd in rear of his brakevan when the express passed him.

Conditions: Dark, with average visibility.

Formation: *The express* — ex-Caledonian Railway 4-4-0 No 14435 (pilot) and Standard compound 4-4-0 No 1176 and 12 vehicles.
The goods train — ex-Caledonian Railway 4-6-0 No 14631.

Damage: *The express* — both engines overturned down an embankment. The leading vehicle, a guard's van, pivoted sideways; the second vehicle, also a guard's van and the next four coaches, were derailed. All vehicles suffered some damage.

Casualties: All four enginemen of the express were killed. The express was lightly loaded and there were no casualties among the passengers.

Signalling: Absolute block with semaphore signalling. Tyer's two-position semaphore block instruments were in use.

Possible safety measures: Some form of lock-and-block signalling to prevent the signalman from accepting a second train until the first one is proved to have passed through the section. Several such systems existed. The use of flares by the guard to warn the driver of a following train of the obstruction was suggested but not adopted.

BETWEEN BEATTOCK SOUTH AND WAMPHRAY
3.20am Wednesday 6 October 1971

Location: Up main line, at 37 miles 1,438yd from Carlisle.

A goods train, No 8Z26, had almost descended Beattock Bank and was running under clear signals at about 35mph when it was run into at the rear with great force by a following goods train, No 6V51, which had become out of control on the steep falling gradient and was travelling at very high speed, probably in excess of 80mph.

Cause: The traincrew of No 6V51 had omitted to carry out an airbrake continuity test before leaving Motherwell. This test is intended to satisfy the traincrew that the brakes are operating on the whole train. They were not, on this occasion, because some of the brake cocks at the ends of vehicles were closed, preventing any brakes further along the train from operating. The staff at Motherwell yard were not free from blame. The airbrake was a relatively new system and it is possible that the training arrangements were inadequate.

Conditions: Dark and clear, with some drizzle.

Formation: *Train No 8Z26, the 00.30 from Dalzell New Yard, Motherwell, to Carlisle* — diesel-electric locomotives Nos 5100 and 8568, with 34 wagons and a brakevan. The continuous brake was in operation on the first 12 wagons. The train was loaded with steel plates and joists.
Train No 6V51, the 01.40 from Dalzell New Yard, Motherwell to Margam — diesel-electric locomotive No 1836 and 24 wagons, each one loaded with two rolled steel coils. Maximum speed 60mph.

Damage: Very destructive. At least 17 wagons were thrown sideways, and many more were derailed. The locomotive of No 6V51 was thrown on its side and caught fire. In all, 26 wagons were damaged beyond repair and 17 were heavily damaged.

Casualties: The guard of the first train was killed.

Possible safety measures: Better training and supervision of train preparation duties.

SOUTH OF BEATTOCK SUMMIT
6.20am Sunday 18 May 1969

Location: On the down main line just south of Harthope Viaduct between Greskine and Beattock Summit signalboxes, at 46 miles 1,577yd from Carlisle.

The 21.30 sleeping car express from Euston to Inverness came to a stand in section between Greskine and Beattock Summit signalboxes when its diesel-electric locomotive was overpowered. Assistance was provided by the following train, the 22.15 sleeping car express from Euston to Glasgow (which was already being assisted by the Beattock bank engine) and it was brought up to the rear of the failed train. Shortly after the Glasgow train started to push the Inverness train, the latter pulled away slightly, creating a gap of a few yards. After travelling about 400yd the Inverness train came suddenly to a stand and was run into by the Glasgow train at about 10mph.

Cause: After the Inverness train pulled clear of the Glasgow train, the locomotive developed wheelslip and lost speed. The driver of the Glasgow train was unable to stop quickly enough.

Conditions: Daylight, but cold with sleet showers.

Formations: *The Inverness train* — Class 50 diesel-electric locomotive and 14 vehicles, including six sleepers.
The Glasgow train — Class 50 diesel-electric locomotive and 12 vehicles, including five sleepers.

Damage: The body of the rear coach of the Inverness train became embedded in the cab of the locomotive of the Glasgow train.

Casualties: The driver of the Glasgow train was killed and the second man was injured, though not seriously.

Possible safety measures: Assisting trains should be coupled to disabled trains, and the brake pipes connected. This was subsequently adopted.

SOUTH OF BEATTOCK SUMMIT
shortly before 5pm Thursday 8 June 1950

Location: 100yd beyond Harthope Viaduct.

The 11am express passenger train from Birmingham New Street to Glasgow Central came to a stand between Greskine and Beattock Summit signalboxes when the communication cord was pulled because a coach (second from the engine) was on fire.

Cause: It is probable that before the train reached Carlisle a cigarette-end was thrown under a seat and caused a slow smouldering of rubbish and a build-up of inflammable gases in an empty compartment whose sliding doors were closed, resulting ultimately in a fireball when the fire burnt a hole through into the next compartment, whose sliding doors were open.

Formation: Class 6P 4-6-0 and 10 coaches.

Damage: Two coaches, the second and third in the train (respectively a corridor composite No 4851, built by the LMS at Wolverton in 1947, and a corridor first No 1073, built by the LMS at Wolverton in 1938) were burnt out.

Casualties: Five passengers were killed.

Possible safety measures: Detail improvements in carriage design to allow easier cleaning underneath seats to remove rubbish, and the provision of fireproofing in that area.

CRAWFORD
9.30pm Friday 2 April 1909

Location: About six miles north of Beattock Summit, near Milepost 56.

As the 2pm express passenger train from Euston to Glasgow was running easily down the bank from Beattock Summit at about 60mph, the entire train became derailed.

Cause: A broken crank axle on the engine, Caledonian Railway 'Cardean' class 4-6-0 No 903. The driving wheel became detached and ran up the side of a cutting. The coupling between the engine and tender broke, the shock derailing the tender, which led the train into derailment.

Formation: Engine and nine coaches.

Damage: The coupling between the engine and tender broke, and the engine ran on for ¾-mile. The tender and all nine coaches were derailed.

Casualties: Only one serious injury.

Possible safety measures: A redesign to avoid a sharp angle between the axle journal and the wheel set, which was a source of problems.

ABINGTON
5.31pm Saturday 8 August 1953

Location: About eight miles north of Beattock Summit and less than a mile beyond Abington station.

The 10am 'Royal Scot' from Euston to Glasgow was descending the bank from Beattock Summit at about 60mph, when it became derailed.

Cause: The track buckled as the train passed over it.

Conditions: Continuous sunshine and unusually warm.

Formation: 'Princess Coronation' class Pacific No 46231 *Duchess of Atholl* and 13 BR Mk 1 bogie vehicles.

Damage: The last seven vehicles became derailed. The damage was remarkably slight, although the last four vehicles lost their bogies.

Casualties: None serious.

Track: The initial derailment occurred on bull-headed track, 32yd beyond the point where a section of 113lb flat-bottomed track was laid. Heavy stresses had built up in the bull-head rail caused by creep and expansion of the stronger flat-bottomed rail pressing forward powerfully against it. These stresses caused the track to buckle as the train passed over.

Possible safety measures: The lessons learned from this accident, about the stresses created where different types of track abut, were applied elsewhere.

AT WISHAW, AND BETWEEN THERE AND MOTHERWELL
4.3pm Friday 5 August 1938

Location: Down line in Wishaw station, and at Motherwell Colliery signalbox.

The 10.25am special goods train from Carlisle to Newton got out of control on the long, falling gradient of about eight miles, and ran away. It crashed into the rear of the 4.5pm passenger train from Wishaw South to Glasgow, which was standing in the station waiting for departure time, at about 20mph. The driver of the passenger train, who was alone on the footplate, saw the runaway train approaching and opened the regulator in an attempt to ease the force of the collision. He was thrown off the footplate by its force. His engine became uncoupled owing to the impact and it ran forward under steam, reaching a speed of almost 60mph. Eventually, after running 3½ miles, it crashed into the rear of the 4.5pm passenger train from Motherwell to Glasgow, which was travelling at 25mph, at Motherwell Colliery signalbox. The engine of that train also became uncoupled and ran forward a short distance, but fortunately the crew remained on board and they were able to stop it.

Cause: The goods train was too heavy for the available braking power, owing to an error by the guard.

Formations: *The goods train* — ex-Caledonian Railway Class 2P 4-4-0 No 14357, with 45 unbraked wagons.

The 4.5pm passenger train from Wishaw — ex-Caledonian Railway Class 3F 0-6-0 No 17594 and five bogie coaches.

The 4.5pm passenger train from Motherwell — ex-Caledonian Railway Class 2F 0-6-0 No 17395 and five bogie coaches.

Damage: *The first collision* — the last coach of the passenger train was badly damaged. There was no derailment, but there was some damage to the goods train engine.

The second collision — the runaway engine was damaged. There was no derailment but the last coach was partly wrecked.

Casualties: The guard of the Motherwell train was killed and the assistant guard was injured. There were no serious injuries to passengers.

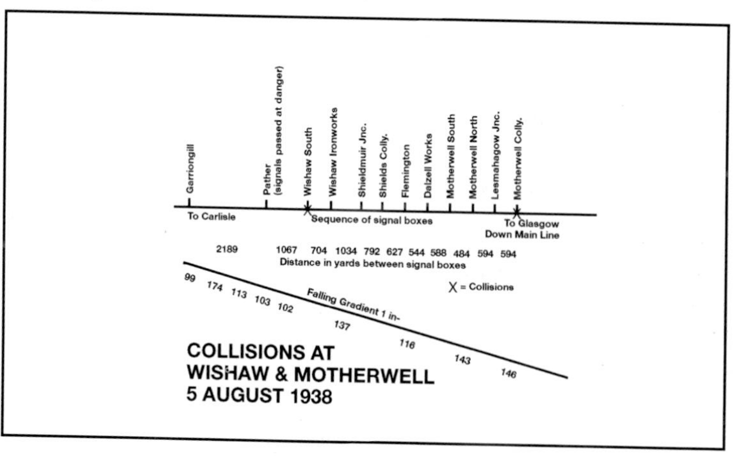

MOTHERWELL
4.31pm Sunday 15 June 1986

Location: At Lesmahagow Junction, approx 150yd north of the up main line Platform 2.

The 16.10 express passenger train from Glasgow to Euston, running under clear signals at over 75mph, became derailed under the fourth coach just north of Motherwell station.

Cause: The track buckled during the passage of the train owing to stresses having built up in the rails following previous engineering work.

Conditions: Very hot. The rail temperature reading on the shady side was 114° F.

Formation: Class 87 electric locomotive, bogie brakevan, and nine coaches.

Damage: The trailing bogie of the fourth vehicle became derailed and the train divided between that coach and the fifth. All the following coaches were derailed, some receiving severe external damage. They came to rest between Platforms 1 and 2 at the station.

Casualties: 12 injured passengers were taken to hospital but only two were detained overnight.

Track: Flat-bottomed continuously-welded rail. Work had been carried out in the area the previous February, but de-stressing had not been carried out afterwards as it was not thought at the time to be necessary.

Possible safety measures: The lessons learned from this accident were applied throughout BR.

UDDINGSTON
9.29pm Monday 17 June 1957

Location: Trailing crossover at Uddingston Junction.

The 1.30pm express passenger train from Euston to Glasgow became derailed whilst travelling at moderate speed.

Cause: It had been necessary to isolate a defective brake cylinder at Carlisle, but the carriage examiner had omitted to release the brake first. The wheels, which were at the front of the leading bogie on the fifth coach, were therefore locked, and during the onward journey a groove had been worn in the middle of the tyre, creating a lip on the outside edge which damaged a wing rail as it passed through a trailing crossover, causing the following coaches to become derailed.

Formation: 'Princess Coronation' class Pacific No 46235 *City of* Bir*mingham* and 12 vehicles. Vacuum braked.

Damage: Six coaches were derailed, the last two being severely damaged in sidelong collision with wagons on an adjoining line.

Casualties: One passenger was killed. Four passengers and the guard were injured.

NEWTON
9.56pm Sunday 21 July 1991

Location: Just north of Newton station on the suburban line, at the point where it was a single bi-directional line.

A few moments after the 21.55 passenger train from Newton to Glasgow had started from the platform it met head-on the 20.55 passenger train from Balloch to Motherwell, at a combined speed of about 60mph.

Cause: The 21.55 from Newton had started past signal M145 at danger at the end of the platform.

Conditions: Clear, dry and dusk.

Formations: *The 21.55 from Newton* — a Class 303 three-car electric multiple-unit (EMU). It carried few passengers.

The 20.55 from Balloch — a Class 314 three-car electric multiple-unit.

Damage: The leading vehicles of both trains were almost completely destroyed.

Casualties: Both drivers and two passengers were killed. A total of 22 passengers were injured, of whom four were detained in hospital.

Signalling: Track circuit block. Multiple-aspect colour-light signalling with continuous track circuiting. AWS installed. Controlled from Motherwell power signalbox.

Track: The original layout consisted of double running junctions between the West Coast main line

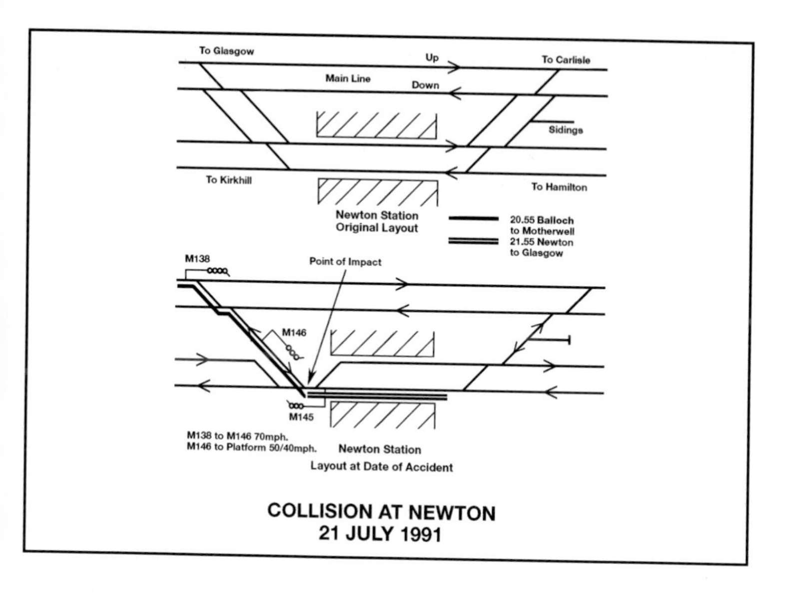

COLLISION AT NEWTON
21 JULY 1991

and the suburban line, at both ends of Newton station. In order to achieve higher speeds on the West Coast main line, the layout was simplified and the double running junctions were converted to single bi-directional connecting lines. After the accident, the layout at the north end of Newton station was modified to eliminate the possibility of a recurrence of the accident.

Possible safety measures: Avoid common sections of bi-directional single line in junction layouts. Install special safety equipment, or introduce special signalling regulations or electrical controls at locations where there is a high risk of serious collision if a signal at danger at the end of a station platform were to be passed erroneously by a train. Install an Automatic Train Protection system.

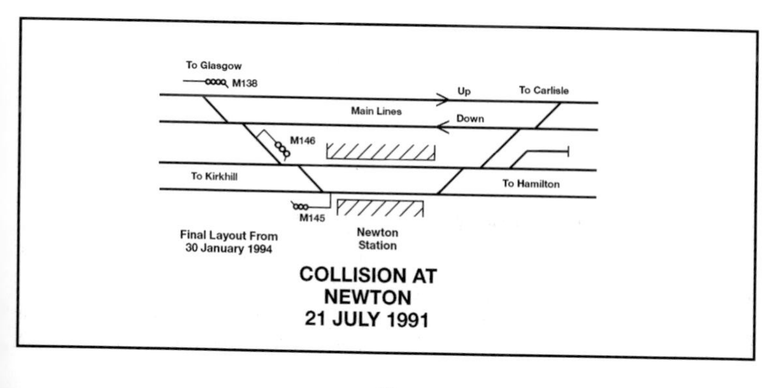

COLLISION AT NEWTON
21 JULY 1991

2 — EAST COAST MAIN LINE

King's Cross to Edinburgh Waverley and Glasgow Queen Street

KING'S CROSS
6.11pm Sunday 4 February 1945

Location: Between the north end of the platforms and the tunnel mouth, on No 1 down main line.

The 6pm express passenger train from King's Cross to Leeds and Bradford left King's Cross and entered Gas Works Tunnel (the centre tunnel) on No 1 down main line. The engine slipped badly on the 1 in 105 rising gradient and slipped to a stand near the north end of the tunnel. It then started to move back at 6-7mph, and as it emerged from the south end of the tunnel it was seen by a signalman in King's Cross signalbox to be running towards Platform 10, in which the coaches of the 7pm to Aberdeen were standing. He switched some points to divert the coaches into Platform 15, which was empty, but unfortunately he was just too late and the point blades moved between the bogies of the leading coach, derailing it. The backward movement of the train forced the coach against a signal bridge stanchion, badly damaging the coach.

Cause: The engine was unable to maintain adhesion with its heavy train, and the driver did not appreciate that the train was actually slipping backwards, owing to steam, smoke and the noise in the tunnel.

Formation: Class A4 Pacific No 2512 *Silver Fox* and 17 bogie vehicles.

Damage: The rear coach, a brake composite, was derailed and forced against a signal bridge steel stanchion, destroying a first class compartment.

Casualties: Two passengers were killed.

Possible safety measures: This was a heavy wartime train. Better tunnel lighting would have enabled the driver to appreciate that he was slipping backwards, and he could then have braked to a stand and sought assistance.

WOOD GREEN STATION
5.30pm Tuesday 29 August 1944

Location: Shortly after passing through the station.

The 5.21pm passenger train from Finsbury Park to Bowes Park became derailed at a speed of 25-30mph when negotiating the junction from down slow No 2 line to the Hertford branch. It was not booked to stop at Wood Green.

Cause: Excessive speed. There was a permanent speed restriction of 15mph.

Conditions: Fine and clear.

Formation: Class N2 0-6-2T No 2675 and eight coaches (two four-coach articulated 'Quad' sets).

Damage: The engine overturned and the first 'Quad' set fell against the adjoining goods line.

Casualties: The enginemen and four passengers were injured.

Possible safety measures: Redesign of track layout.

Right: **NEW SOUTHGATE 17 July 1948**
Two breakdown cranes are seen rerailing *Duke of Rothesay*, closely observed by a group of raincoated officials.
F. R. Hebron/IAL

NEW SOUTHGATE
6am Saturday 17 July 1948

Location: The derailment started near Milepost 7¾.

As the 7.50pm sleeping car express from Edinburgh to King's Cross was passing through the short tunnel north of New Southgate at about 70mph, the trailing bogie wheels of the engine became derailed. When the engine reached a 'V' crossing 689yd ahead, outside the tunnel, the leading bogie wheels also became derailed and destroyed the track, resulting in the whole train becoming derailed.

Cause: Defective track. There was a high rail-joint, combined with irregular cross-level.

Formation: Class A2/1 Pacific No 60508 *Duke of Rothesay* and 11 bogie vehicles including a sleeping car.

Damage: The engine turned over and slid on its side. The leading vehicle was also overturned and badly damaged.

Casualties: The fireman was killed, but there were no serious injuries among the passengers.

Track: Laid new in 1936 and rerailed in 1944 with 95lb bull-head rails.

Possible safety measures: Improved maintenance standards.

POTTERS BAR
between 10.8pm and 10.10pm Sunday 10 February 1946

Location: North end of Potters Bar station, up and down main lines.

The 9.32pm local passenger train from Hatfield to King's Cross approached Potters Bar station on the up slow line. As the slow line ended north of the station it was necessary to divert it through a crossover road on to the up main line prior to its station stop, but it had to wait until the 5pm express passenger train from Bradford Exchange to King's Cross had passed. The signalbox at Potters Bar was situated immediately north of the down platform and the signalman saw the local train approaching at too high a speed and passing his inner home signal at danger. He was concerned that it would collide with the buffer stops in the dead-end and become derailed, possibly fouling the main lines on which expresses were approaching; therefore he put his signals back to danger against the expresses and reversed his crossover in an attempt to divert the local train on to the up main line. Unfortunately he was not quick enough and he moved the points between the bogies of the first coach, causing it and the second coach to become derailed. Both main lines were blocked and a minute later the 9.45pm express passenger train from King's Cross to Edinburgh ran into the wreckage at about 45mph. A few seconds later the 5pm from Bradford ran into the wreckage at low speed, 5-10mph.

Cause: Though there were conflicts of evidence, it was concluded that the driver of the local passenger train had wrongly passed the inner home signal at danger. In a moment of mistaken zeal the signalman attempted to move the crossover in front of the local train, but he did so a little too late.

Conditions: It was a clear night.

Formations: *The local train* — Class N2 0-6-2T No 2679 and two quadruple inner-suburban sets. It carried 30 passengers.
The up express — Class V2 2-6-2 No 4833 and 10 coaches. It carried about 450 passengers.
The down express — Class V2 2-6-2 No 4876, 12 bogie vehicles and a six-wheeled van. It carried 595 passengers.

Damage: *The local train* — the first three coaches were wrecked and the fourth badly damaged (the tank engine, which ran forward into the buffers, was hardly damaged).
The up express — the engine and tender were turned over on to their sides. There was little damage to the train.
The down express — the tender was overturned and the first six coaches were derailed. The first coach was considerably damaged.

Casualties: Two passengers in the Hatfield train were killed and 11 others, together with six railway staff, from all three trains, were injured or suffered from shock.

Signalling: Semaphore signals and an up main line outer colour-light distant. There were both up main and up slow inner and outer home signals. There was extensive track-circuiting, except between the inner home signals and the starting signals below. Operation to the next signalboxes was by train-describing bell.

Possible safety measures: The provision of a track circuit and electric locking to prevent the signalman from moving the facing points up slow/up main after the train has passed the up slow inner home signal. Various signalling controls were subsequently installed.

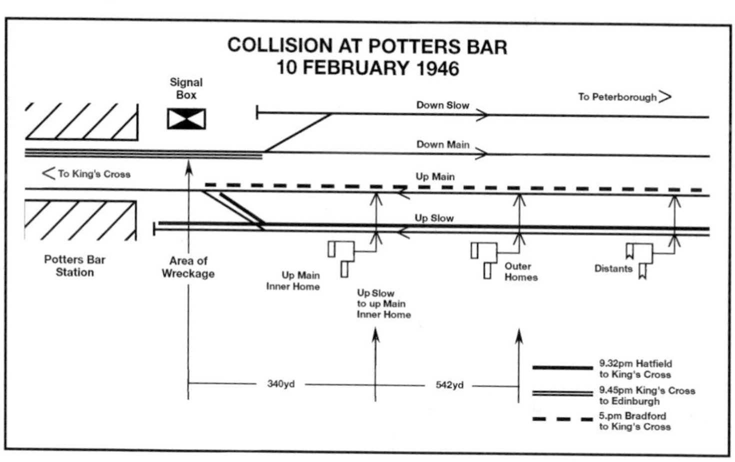

HATFIELD
7.30pm Monday 15 July 1946

Location: Down main line approaching Hatfield, 200yd beyond Milepost 17 and 700yd south of Hatfield No 1 signalbox.

The 7.5pm express passenger train from King's Cross to Aberdeen was approaching Hatfield on the down main line at about 60mph when the whole train became derailed except for the leading pony wheels and the rear bogie of the last vehicle.

Cause: Track irregularities.

Conditions: Cool and showery.

Formation: Class V2 2-6-2 No 3645 and 14 bogie vehicles. The train conveyed nearly 400 passengers.

Damage: The first three vehicles overturned and were scattered. The engine and tender ran forward and remained upright.

Casualties: Eleven passengers were injured.

Track: Resleepered and rechaired 15 days earlier. The rails were 60ft bull-head, eight years old. The existing ballast was riddled and reused. There was a 2¾in cant on the curve. The temporary speed restriction imposed after this work was removed four days before the accident.

Possible safety measures: There were some slight variations in cant levels, but the pony truck of the 'V2' engines was known to be a contributory factor in a derailment.

HATFIELD
10.9am Thursday 26 January 1939

Location: Up main line between Welwyn Garden City and Hatfield, about ¾-mile north of Hatfield, almost beneath overbridge No 63.

There had been a heavy snowfall which had brought down the telegraph wires and as a result of this there was no communication between Welwyn Garden City and Hatfield No 2 signalboxes. Trains were therefore being worked under the 'time-interval' system, and drivers were so advised and cautioned before entering the section. During this period the 7.15am passenger train from Peterborough to King's Cross ran into the rear of the 8.25am passenger train from Cambridge to King's Cross at 30-35mph. The latter was standing in a queue of four trains waiting to pass through Hatfield, and the force of the collision drove it forward into the train in front — the 7.34am passenger train from Cambridge to King's Cross, which was standing 25yd ahead of it.

Cause: The 7.15am from Peterborough travelled through the section at too high a speed.

Conditions: The snow had ceased falling, and visibility was good.

Formations: *7.15am from Peterborough —*

Above: **HATFIELD 26 January 1939**
Scene of the accident looking south, with 'V2' No 4813 embedded in the rear of the 8.25am from Cambridge, whose two rear carriages lie shattered across the adjacent lines. ***Hulton-Deutsch***

Class V2 2-6-2 No 4813 and nine bogie vehicles.
8.25am from Cambridge — Class C1 Atlantic No 4437 and 11 bogie vehicles.
7.34am from Cambridge —Class B17 'Sandringham' 4-6-0 No 2840 *Somerleyton Hall* and 10 bogie vehicles.

Damage: The last two coaches of the 8.25am from Cambridge were destroyed.

Casualties: One passenger in the Cambridge train was killed. Five injured passengers were detained in hospital and there were many minor injuries.

Signalling: Absolute block with semaphore signals, but normal working was suspended at the time.

Possible safety measures: Drivers, after having been cautioned, must travel at such a speed as will enable them to stop safely well clear of any obstruction. Failure to do this was a common cause of accidents for many years before this accident, and for many years after.

WELWYN GARDEN CITY
7.12am Monday 7 January 1957

Location: Up main line just beyond the up advanced starting signal.

The 7.10pm sleeping car express from Aberdeen to King's Cross, travelling at 60-65mph, overtook and collided with the rear of the 6.18am passenger train from Baldock to King's Cross, which was running at 30-35mph.

Cause: Although there was contradictory evidence, it was concluded that the driver of the express failed to observe the signals at Welwyn Garden City, all of which were against him, and failed to react to the explosion of the emergency detonators at the signalbox. He wrongly entered the section ahead (the advanced starting signal was still at clear but it was in that position for the train from Baldock). The driver maintained that the up outer distant signal was clear, but admitted that he saw neither the outer nor the inner home signals, nor did he hear the detonators explode.

Conditions: Misty, with dawn breaking.

Formations: *The Baldock train* — Class L1 2-6-4T No 67741 and six coaches.
The express — Class A2/3 Pacific No 60520 *Owen Tudor* and 11 bogie vehicles.

Damage: *The Baldock train* — the last two coaches were overturned, the rear one being wrecked. *The express* — the engine turned over on to its side.

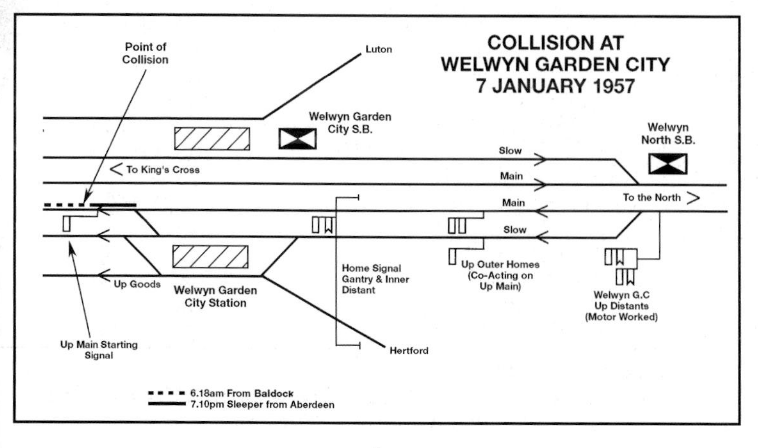

60520

Casualties: One passenger in the local train was killed and five injured passengers were detained in hospital after the first day.

Signalling: Absolute block with semaphore signals. Interlocking block was in use, and no train could be accepted on the up line unless the arms of the outer distant signals were in the caution position. AWS equipment had been provided on the track, but the express engine had not yet been equipped.

Possible safety measures: AWS. Subsequently, the outer distant semaphore signals were replaced with colour-light signals. It was recommended that more powerful detonators be used in signalbox emergency machines.

Left: **WELWYN GARDEN CITY 7 January 1957**
Pacific No 60520 lies on its side with its derailed train behind it and still in line, after it overtook and collided with the 6.18am from Baldock. ***Hulton-Deutsch***

WELWYN GARDEN CITY
11.27pm Saturday 15 June 1935

Location: On the down main line a few yards north of the signalbox, which was located a few yards north of the down platform.

The 10.58pm express passenger train from King's Cross to Leeds Central, travelling at not less than 65mph, overtook and collided violently with the rear of the 10.53pm express passenger train from King's Cross to Newcastle, which was recovering from a signal check and travelling at about 20mph.

Cause: The evidence in this case is not clear, but it appears that the signalman at Welwyn Garden City became confused and wrongly assumed that the Newcastle express had passed his signalbox whilst in fact it was still in the rear section from Hatfield No 3 signalbox. His down main line signals were at danger because he had omitted to clear them for the Newcastle express, but in his confusion he appears to have assumed that he had cleared them and then replaced them after that train had passed. He therefore sent the 'Train out of Section' signal to Hatfield No 3 signalbox and was immediately offered, and accepted, the Leeds express. He had already obtained a 'Line Clear' from Welwyn North signalbox and he therefore cleared all his signals. Alternatively, he may in error have given the 'Train

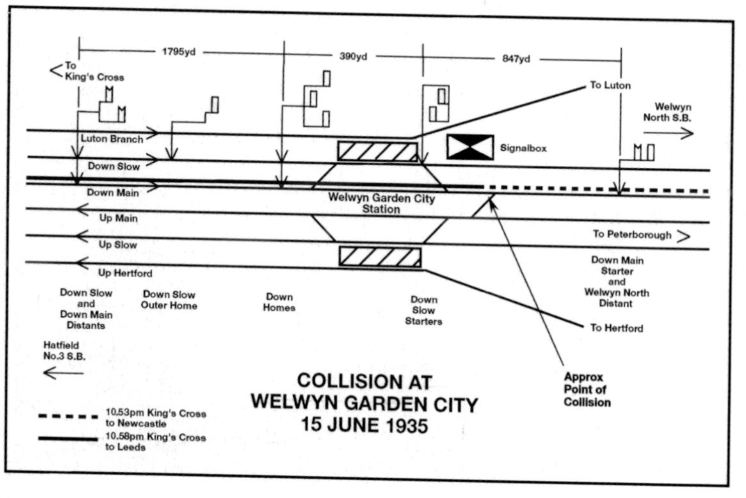

out of Section' signal to Hatfield No 3 signalbox for an up train.

In the event, when the down line signals were cleared, the Newcastle express was about halfway between the distant and home signals, and the driver drew forward at about 20mph until he saw the starting signal. He was starting to accelerate when the collision occurred.

Conditions: Dark and drizzly, but reasonable visibility.

Formations: *The Newcastle train* — Class C1 Atlantic 4-4-2 No 4441, brakevan and 10 bogie coaches. It conveyed 280 passengers.
The Leeds train — Class K3 2-6-0 No 4009 and 11 bogie vehicles, marshalled brakevan, two coaches, three vans, a coach, and four vans. It conveyed 57 passengers.

Damage: *The Newcastle train* — the rear coach, a third class brake, was completely shattered and the next coach was badly damaged at the rear end.
The Leeds train — the engine was damaged but not derailed. The three vans were wrecked and the following coach, a composite brake, was partly telescoped by the following van.

Casualties: 13 passengers, and the guard of the Newcastle train, were killed, whilst 29 passengers were injured and detained in hospital.

Signalling: Absolute block with semaphore signals.

Possible safety measures: Apparatus to prevent the signalman from accepting a second train until the preceding train has been proved to have passed through the section. This was achieved at Welwyn Garden City by requiring the berth track circuit in rear of the down home signal to be occupied and then cleared before the block indicator could again be placed at 'Line Clear'. Special release apparatus was provided for use during failures of equipment, etc. The system became known as 'Welwyn Control'. Equipment providing a similar function had been in use elsewhere for many years.

Above: **WELWYN GARDEN CITY 15 June 1935**
The scene of the accident, looking south to the station. The signalbox can be seen to the right of the breakdown cranes. Note the green fields surrounding the station. *NRM*

HITCHIN
4.30am Wednesday 19 November 1958

Location: 140yd beyond the down main outer home signal.

The 2.28am goods train from London to Peterborough was just beginning to move forward from Hitchin South signalbox's down main inner home signals, after the driver had stopped there to ascertain the position of the signals in the thick fog, when it was run into in the rear at about 15mph by the 3.25am goods train from London to Peterborough. Some of the first train's wagons were derailed across the up main line and were struck almost immediately by the 10.35pm Class D express goods train from Leeds to London, whose derailed wagons struck a light engine on the adjoining up slow line.

Cause: The driver of the 3.25am down goods had wrongly passed Wymondley down main auto stop signal at danger, and the signalman at Hitchin South was slow in replacing his distant signal, not doing so until it had already been passed by the 3.25am train.

Conditions: Variable fog and mist, with conditions deteriorating. The fog signalmen had been sent for 10min before the collision.

Formations: *The 2.28am train* — BR Class 9F 2-10-0, 38 wagons and a brakevan.
The 3.25am train — BR Class 9F 2-10-0, 47 wagons and a brakevan.
The 10.35pm train — ex-LNER Class V2 2-6-2, 27 wagons and brakevan (18 vacuum fitted).
The light engine — ex-LNER Class L1 2-6-4T.

Damage: *The 2.28 train* — the fifth to the eighth wagons were thrown across on to the up main line. The last seven wagons and the brakevan were derailed and badly damaged.
The 3.25am train — the engine was derailed, but the train was virtually undamaged.
The 10.35pm train — the engine and 17 wagons were derailed or badly damaged.
The light engine — overturned on to its side.

Casualties: Several members of the traincrews were slightly injured.

Signalling: The signalbox in rear was Stevenage North, and there was an automatic section, known as Wymondley, between that signalbox and Hitchin South. The Wymondley outer and inner distants were both colour-light signals, but the automatic stop signal was a semaphore, normally in the clear position. The down main line outer distant at Hitchin was a colour-light signal capable of showing two yellows, but the inner distant and the home signals were all semaphores.

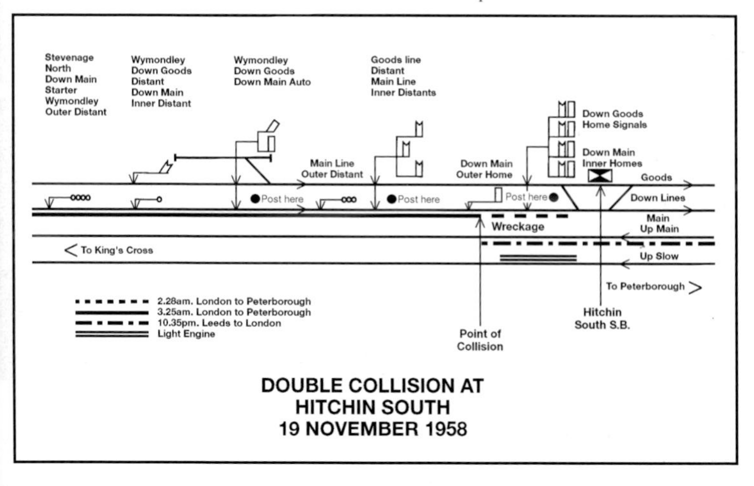

DOUBLE COLLISION AT HITCHIN SOUTH 19 NOVEMBER 1958

Possible safety measures: AWS track equipment was already in place, but the engines had not yet been equipped. It was recommended that the Wymondley down main automatic stop signal, a semaphore, be replaced by a three-aspect colour-light signal incorporating Hitchin South down main outer distant signal.

BETWEEN BARFORD AND ST NEOTS
2.3am Thursday 18 March 1937

Location: ¾-mile south of St Neots signalbox.

The 10.20pm express passenger train from York to King's Cross was travelling under clear signals at 65-70mph when the rear vehicle, a four-wheeled 9ft wheelbase fishvan, became derailed and uncoupled. It came to rest foul of the down main line, and was struck by the second part of the 1.10am sleeping car express from King's Cross to Newcastle, which was travelling at 70mph.

Cause: 9ft wheelbase four-wheeled vans were prone to derailment at over 60mph. The van concerned had a tare weight of 9½ tons and a load of two tons.

Formations: *The train from York* — Class K3 2-6-0 No 2451, 12 bogie vehicles and two four-wheeled fishvans. It conveyed only 20 passengers.

The train to Newcastle — Class C1 Atlantic No 4450 and nine vehicles. It conveyed 56 passengers.

Damage: There was some damage to the Newcastle engine and minor damage to the first two vehicles.

Casualties: The driver of the Newcastle express was killed.

Possible safety measures: Four-wheeled short-wheelbase vehicles have always been prone to derailment at high speeds. Over the years some speed restrictions were imposed by the different companies, and the maximum permissible speeds of such vehicles were gradually reduced. They were not allowed to be conveyed on express passenger trains except where specially nominated.

HUNTINGDON
About 5pm Saturday 14 July 1951

Location: About one mile north of the station.

Fire broke out in the second coach of the 3.45pm express passenger train from King's Cross to Leeds as it was travelling at about 55mph.

Cause: It is likely that the fire was started when a piece of live coal from the engine became lodged in a small hole, from which the packing was missing, in the underside of the coach at an airduct. It smouldered and eventually burst into flame, assisted by flammable materials used in the internal decoration and finish of the coach.

Conditions: Fine and warm.

Formation: Class A3 Pacific No 60058 *Blair Atholl* and 14 coaches, marshalled three open twins and eight corridor coaches. There were 10 first class and 337 third class passengers.

Damage: The bodies of the four leading coaches were completely destroyed. The coach in which the fire broke out was one of a twin-set built to a high standard of luxury by the LNER for the 1937 high-speed trains. The whole of the interior was covered with a nitrocellulose coated fabric, a type of leather-cloth known as 'Rexine', which was found to be highly combustible.

Casualties: Nine passengers and the guard were detained in hospital with burns or other injuries.

Possible safety measures: Avoid using flammable materials in the interior finish of coaches. Following this accident remedial work was carried out on the entire coaching stock fleet. The provision of an additional outside door in the centre of open coaches to speed up evacuation was incorporated in the new construction of open coaches for several years.

BETWEEN CONNINGTON AND ABBOTS RIPTON
Between 10.15pm and 10.23pm Friday 15 December 1961

Location: About 1½ miles south of Connington South signalbox.

A Class C (fully-fitted) express goods train had been signalled on to the up goods line at Connington South to follow an unfitted Class H goods train, and it was travelling at about 10mph in thick fog when it was run into in the rear by an empty coaching stock train travelling at about 30mph. The brakevan of the Class C goods train was thrown on to the adjoining up main line foul of the down main line. Some 3-4min later a Class C express goods train, travelling on the down main line at about 50mph, struck the brakevan a glancing blow, and 3-4min after that another Class C express goods train travelling on the up main line at about 35mph ran into the wreckage.

Cause: The empty coaching stock train was being driven at too high a speed in the prevailing weather conditions.

Conditions: Dark, with thick fog.

Formations: *The Class C goods train on the up goods line* — the 9.50pm from New England to King's Cross — Class V2 2-6-2 No 60803 and 24 wagons and brakevan.
The empty coaching stock train — the 9.55am from Scotswood (Newcastle) to Holloway (London) — 'Deltic' diesel-electric No D9012 and nine vans.
The Class C goods train on the down main line — the 8.10pm from King's Cross Goods to Newcastle — Class A3 Pacific No 60078 *Night Hawk*, 34 wagons and a brakevan.
The Class C goods train on the up main line — the 10.5am Aberdeen to King's Cross Goods — Class V2 2-6-2 No 60977 with 25 vans and a brakevan.

Damage: In the first collision the brakevan and two vehicles of the 9.50pm train were wrecked. The 'Deltic' and two vans were derailed. In the subsequent collisions both steam engines on the main lines were turned over, and of the 61 wagons on the two trains, 28 were wrecked and 11 more were derailed or damaged.

Casualties: Two enginemen and a guard were injured and detained in hospital for a day or two.

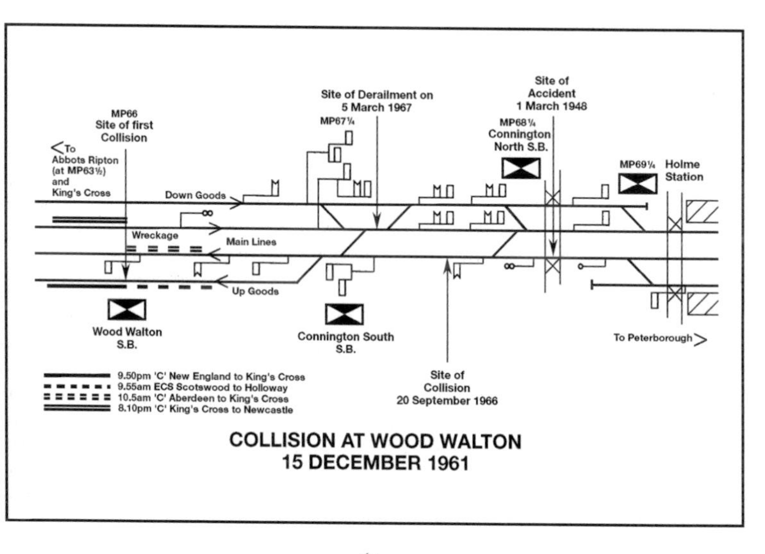

COLLISION AT WOOD WALTON
15 DECEMBER 1961

Signalling: There are up and down main lines north of Connington South signalbox, but south thereof there were up and down goods lines on the outside of the main lines. The goods lines were worked on the permissive block system, allowing more than one goods train to be in the section to Abbots Ripton at the same time. On the main lines the signals were a mixture of colour-light and semaphore, but the goods line signals were exclusively semaphore. There was no separate signal at Connington South to indicate to a driver entering the up goods line that there was already a train (or more than one) in the section ahead of him to Abbots Ripton, nearly four miles away.

Possible safety measures: A separate 'calling-on' signal at Connington South would have given a positive indication to a driver of the state of the goods line ahead and ought to have been provided. The use of permissive block on goods lines adjoining the high speed East Coast main line was, in some respects, a relic of the past by 1961, and was eventually abandoned. Its use during fog was especially hazardous.

CONNINGTON SOUTH
11.36pm Sunday 5 March 1967

Location: Facing points in the down main line giving access to the down goods line.

As the 22.30 sleeping car express from King's Cross to Edinburgh was passing over the points under clear signals at a speed of about 75mph the rear portion of the train became derailed.

Cause: The points were moved irregularly by the signalman as the train was passing over them.

Conditions: Dark and clear.

Formation: 'Deltic' diesel-electric No D9004 and 11 vehicles, marshalled as follows: brakevan, three Post Office sorting vans, sleeping car, five corridor coaches, brakevan.

Damage: The train divided between the seventh and eighth coaches, the rear four vehicles coming to rest almost on their sides. The sixth and seventh coaches were derailed but remained coupled to the front portion, finally coming to a stand about 600yd further on.

Casualties: Five passengers were killed and 18 were injured, two of them seriously.

Signalling: The facing points were operated manually from Connington South signalbox, and were equipped with a facing point bolt which prevented the points from moving when the controlling lever had been reversed. In addition, there was a track circuit between the junction semaphore home signals and the points, and when it was 'occupied' neither the points lever nor the bolt lever could be moved. These controls were provided to ensure that the points could not move, or be moved, in such a manner as to endanger a train.

Possible safety measures: Initially it was not possible to establish a clear cause of the derailment, but after exhaustive trials and investigations it appears that the facing points were deliberately moved by the signalman as the train was passing over them. He was able to do this by throwing the junction home signal back to danger at the very instant it moved out of the driver's line of sight with the locomotive a few feet from the signal, and 2sec before it reached the track circuit. During those 2sec the signalman unlocked the facing points and freed the points themselves, but he did not move them until half the train had passed over them. He then reversed them and quickly restored them. For this irregular action he was sentenced to two years imprisonment at a trial in November 1968.

BETWEEN CONNINGTON NORTH AND CONNINGTON SOUTH SIGNALBOXES
5.4am Tuesday 20 September 1966

The 22.30 sleeping car express from Edinburgh to King's Cross was brought to a stand at Connington South up home signal by the driver, because a fault had developed in the diesel-electric locomotive. It was then planned to propel it to Abbots Ripton, about four miles to the south, where a fresh locomotive would be attached. A fully-fitted express goods train was already standing at Connington North signalbox, about half a mile away, and it was decided to use this train for the propelling movement. However, whilst this operation was being carried out the goods train ran into the rear of the express at about 6mph.

Cause: The guard of the express went back along the line to the goods train, putting down detonators, but he and the driver of the goods train did not come to a proper understanding of the arrangements to be made to bring the goods train safely to the rear of the passenger train, nor of the precise location of the detonators.

Conditions: Foggy, with visibility about 50yd.

Formations: *The express* — 'Deltic' diesel-electric No D9006 and 13 bogie vehicles, including six sleeping cars.
The goods train — the 22.15 from Tees to Temple Mills — Type 4 diesel-electric No D168, 34 fully-fitted wagons and two brakevans.

Damage: There was no derailment, but all the coaches suffered some damage, and the eighth vehicle, a sleeping car, telescoped slightly into the sleeping car in front.

Casualties: There were no serious injuries, but five passengers were taken to hospital.

Protection: In the prevailing weather conditions the guard decided to put down some detonators as a safeguard, although the rules did not require him to do so. However, he failed to ensure that the driver knew exactly where the detonators were placed, and the driver equally failed to satisfy himself on that point, therefore he was misled as to the exact position of the train in front. In addition, he travelled through the section at too high a speed.

Possible safety measures: The rules for protecting a failed train against the possibility of the assisting train approaching too fast were inadequate, especially during fog, and were subsequently revised to require the use of detonators and other safeguards.

CONNINGTON NORTH
Shortly after 7am Monday 1 March 1948

Location: The up main line at occupation level crossing No 85, 80yd north of Connington North signalbox.

A 2½-ton lorry carrying 11 German prisoners of war from Glatton Camp to work on Glatton and Speechley farms was crossing the line from west to east, when it was struck by a light engine, an 0-6-0 running tender first at about 20mph on the up main line. The lorry had already crossed two lines (a siding and the down main line).

Cause: The lorry driver had failed to ensure that it was safe to cross before doing so.

Conditions: Dense fog. Shortly after sunrise.

Casualties: Three Germans were killed and three more died in hospital. The other five were all seriously injured. The ambulance, after travelling ½-mile, collided with a bus carrying railway staff to the marshalling yard, resulting in a doctor and a medical orderly being injured.

Possible safety measures: Pending a more satisfactory solution, a telephone to the signalbox should be provided. This was a previously quiet level crossing which had become very busy owing to intensive agricultural development during the war, and the unlocked field gates were often left open.

Postscript: At 5.26pm on 16 October the same year, in rain and failing light, a car travelling from east to west was struck and wrecked by an up empty coaching stock train travelling at 50mph. The car driver was killed.

PETERBOROUGH
5.23pm Thursday 1 September 1955

Location: Down main line at Westwood Junction, about ½-mile north of Peterborough North station.

The 3.50pm express passenger train from King's Cross to Leeds had accelerated to about 20mph after the Peterborough station stop, when it became derailed.

Cause: The fracture of the right-hand frame plate of the engine bogie, caused originally by faulty repairs in the main workshops some years earlier.

Formation: Ex-LNER Class W1 4-6-4 engine No 60700 and 13 vehicles.

Damage: The engine and the first coach turned over on to their sides. The second coach was tilted over.

Casualties: Four injured passengers were detained overnight in hospital.

Possible safety measures: Improved standards of maintenance, inspection and design.

GRANTHAM
11.4pm Wednesday 19 September 1906

Location: Down branch line just beyond the junction towards Nottingham, north of the station.

The 8.45pm sleeping car express from King's Cross to Edinburgh approached Grantham with all signals in the clear position worked from Grantham South and Grantham Yard signalboxes, but with Grantham North distant signal at danger. It failed to make its booked station stop at Grantham but passed through the station at 40/50mph. Its driver failed to obey the North signalbox's junction home signals set at danger at the north end of the station and he went past them without significantly reducing speed.

The signalman had set his junction points, 135yd beyond the platform, to allow a goods train from the Nottingham direction to join the up main line, but before he could operate the junction trailing points in the up main line the interlocking required him to reverse the facing points in the down main line and

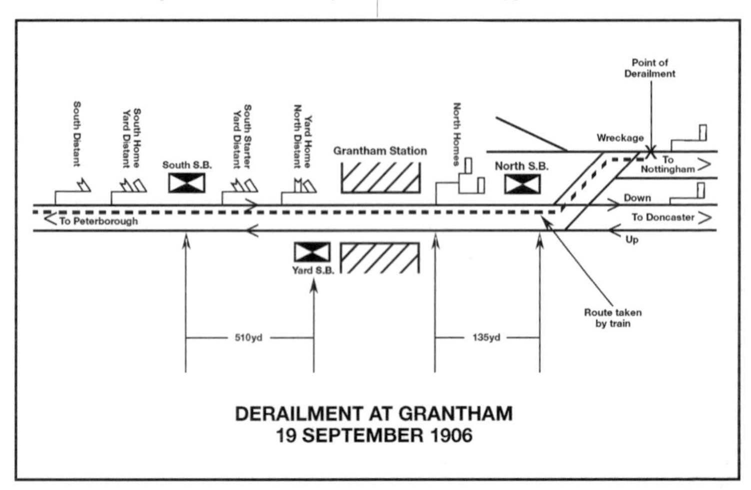

DERAILMENT AT GRANTHAM
19 SEPTEMBER 1906

set them towards Nottingham in order to give 'flank protection', in case a train on the down main line should run past the signals at Grantham North. The sleeping car express did just that, and was diverted through the junction to the Nottingham line. However, there was a speed restriction of 15mph through the junction, but the express was travelling too fast to remain on the lines and it became derailed at the far end of the reverse curves of the junction, plunging down an embankment.

Cause: The driver failed to stop at the signals at Grantham North. The guard realised that the train was going too fast and he went to apply the brake, but vacuum had already been destroyed, presumably by the driver. At this time the train had just reached the platform and the wheels were reported to be skidding and throwing up sparks. The reason why the driver failed to make the booked station stop, and failed to stop at the signal at danger at Grantham North, was never discovered. Both enginemen were killed.

Conditions: Dark and clear.

Formation: Atlantic engine No 276 and 12 vehicles, marshalled four brake and mail vans, two six-wheeled coaches, two 12-wheeled sleeping cars, two 12-wheeled coaches and two brakevans. All but two of the vehicles were gas-lit. It conveyed about 50 passengers.

Damage: The engine overturned, whilst the tender and five vehicles went down the embankment and were wrecked. Four more vehicles were almost completely wrecked. Fire broke out in the wreckage. The last three vehicles were derailed but remained upright.

Casualties: Eleven passengers, a Post Office attendant and the two enginemen were killed.

Signalling: Absolute block with semaphore signals. There was only about 500yd braking distance between the North signalbox's distant and home signals, but there was 700yd sighting distance of the distant signal.

Possible safety measures: Automatic train control could have prevented an accident like this, but its development was in its infancy. It was recommended that the working of the distant signals should be interlocked, so that the Yard signalbox distant signal could not be cleared until the North signalbox distant signal had been cleared.

WESTBOROUGH
3.30pm Monday 28 April 1941

Location: Eight miles north of Grantham and 490yd before reaching Westborough signalbox.

As the second portion of the 12.45pm express passenger train from King's Cross to Newcastle was travelling at about 55mph under clear signals, fire broke out in the last coach but one and the train was stopped by the communication cord being pulled.

Cause: The last three vehicles were two open thirds and a brakevan, and were reserved for about 100 boys returning to Ampleforth College. Some boys had been flicking lighted matches about and one lodged down the side of a seat. Fire broke out.

Formation: Class V2 2-6-2 No 4779 and 11 vehicles. The two coaches concerned were tourist vehicles with bucket-type seats.

Damage: The last three vehicles were burnt out, but they were uncoupled from the remainder of the train, which drew forward.

Casualties: Six boys were killed and seven were injured.

Possible safety measures: None, other than closer supervision of parties of schoolchildren.

NEWARK
8.16pm Monday 6 September 1915

Location: Down main line opposite the station sidings.

The 5.45pm express passenger train from King's Cross was running under clear signals at about 60mph when it struck an empty wagon which had become derailed during shunting operations in the sidings.

Cause: An error during shunting.

Formation: Atlantic engine No 1455 and 11 vehicles. Only one coach was gas-lit. The train conveyed 251 passengers.

Damage: All the carriages were derailed but remained upright, except one, the seventh, which turned over on to its side. The engine and first two coaches came to a stand opposite Newark Midland Crossing signalbox.

Casualties: One passenger was killed and 15 were injured.

RETFORD
5.6am Wednesday 13 February 1923

Location: 550yd north of Retford station, near Milepost 139.

An up sleeping car express from Aberdeen to King's Cross, running at about 60mph, collided with the rear of a Class A goods train, which was just in the process of slowly setting back at Retford North. The goods train had just detached a wagon of cattle.

Cause: The express ran past the home signal at Canal signalbox, 1,223yd before the collision, and the home signal at Babworth, 477yd before the collision.

Conditions: Fairly thick fog.

Formations: *The express* — Atlantic No 298 and 11 vehicles, all electrically-lit, including three 12-wheeled sleeping cars.
The goods train — 0-6-0 No 634, 50 loaded wagons and a brakevan.

Damage: *The express* — the engine and tender turned over on to their sides. The first coach turned over and the second partly so. The third coach was derailed, but remained upright.
The goods train — the brakevan and 16 wagons were destroyed.

Casualties: Both enginemen of the express, and an inspector travelling on the footplate, were killed. Seventeen passengers and six railway staff suffered minor injuries.

Signalling: Absolute block with semaphore signals. There were no detonator placers at the signalboxes.

Possible safety measures: Automatic train control would almost certainly have prevented this accident. There were no emergency detonator-placing machines at either signalbox — they might have alerted the driver to the fact that he was passing a signal in the danger position.

DONCASTER
4.41pm Saturday 9 August 1947

Location: Between Balby Junction and Bridge Junction signalboxes, about ¼-mile south of Doncaster station.

The 1.10pm express passenger train from King's Cross to Leeds had been brought to a stand at Bridge Junction signalbox home signal and was just moving forward when it was run into in the rear at about

40mph by the 1.25pm express passenger train from King's Cross to Leeds, which was running under clear signals.

Cause: Grave errors in block working at Balby Junction signalbox. The signalman wrongly accepted the 1.25pm train from Red Bank signalbox when he did not have the necessary ¼-mile clearance — the 1.10pm train was standing only 177yd ahead of his signalbox. He then improperly allowed the 1.25pm train to enter the section ahead under clear signals, although he could easily have seen the 1.10pm train, and even though he had not received 'Train out of Section' for the 1.10pm and had not had 'Line Clear' for the 1.25pm.

Conditions: Fine with good visibility.

Formation: *The 1.10pm train* — Class A3 Pacific No 50 *Persimmon* and 14 coaches. The train had 470 seats but was crowded and carried about 700 passengers.
The 1.25pm train — Class V2 2-6-2 No 936 and 12 coaches. The train had 629 seats and also carried about 700 passengers.

Damage: *The 1.10pm train* — the last three coaches were destroyed and the next one overturned. *The 1.25pm train* — the engine and tender overturned to the left and the next two coaches were derailed.

Casualties: Seventeen passengers and a railwayman were killed. In all, 51 people were injured and detained in hospital. Many people suffered minor injuries.

Signalling: Absolute block. The down home signal at Balby Junction did not require a 'Line Clear' release and there was no track circuit in rear of it. The two distant signals were worked electrically by the home signal lever. When a bell sounded in Balby Junction signalbox, it indicated that Bridge Junction home signal (four-aspect colour-light) had been cleared, and it authorised the Balby Junction signalman to clear his own distant signals (but only if the train had been accepted by Bridge Junction, which it had not in this accident).

Possible safety measures: A comprehensive resignalling scheme was being developed with modern controls and safeguards.

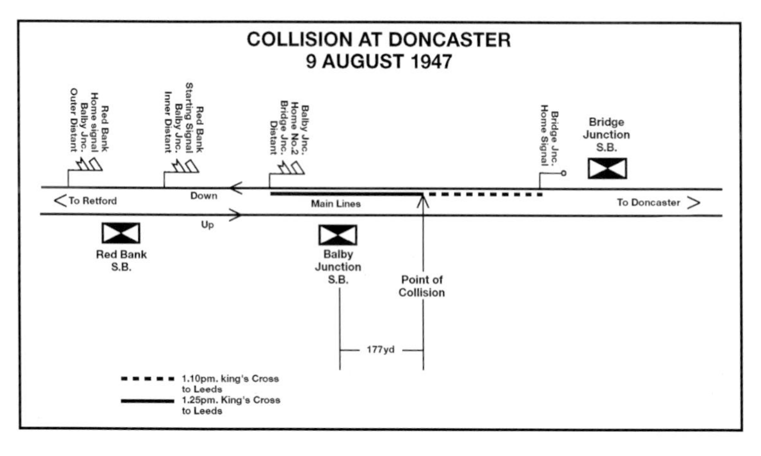

DONCASTER
10.9am Friday 16 March 1951

Location: The derailment occurred at a scissors crossing from the up slow line to the up main line a few hundred yards south of the station, and a derailed coach struck a pier of Balby Bridge about 100yd further along.

The 8.45am express passenger train from Hull and the 9.15am express passenger train from York combined at Doncaster to form the 10.6am to King's Cross, with the Hull portion leading. Shortly after leaving the station the train was derailed.

Cause: The scissors crossing had a speed restriction of 10mph owing to the effect of super-elevation on the main line. The train had accelerated to between 20 and 25mph when the derailment occurred, but it is considered to have been caused by the bursting of the crossing nose, which had not been adequately maintained.

Formation: Class A2/2 Pacific No 60501 *Cock o' the North* with 14 coaches and a horsebox.

Damage: The third coach and the following seven became derailed. The third coach started to follow the front two to the right of a brick pier of Balby Road Bridge, but it became uncoupled and its rear end was pushed to the left of the pier by the momentum of the following coaches, causing it to wrap itself round the pier and be crushed to destruction. The sixth and seventh coaches were also overturned.

Casualties: 14 passengers were killed and 12 were detained in hospital with serious injuries.

Possible safety measures: Higher standards of track maintenance. Fitting engines with speedometers.

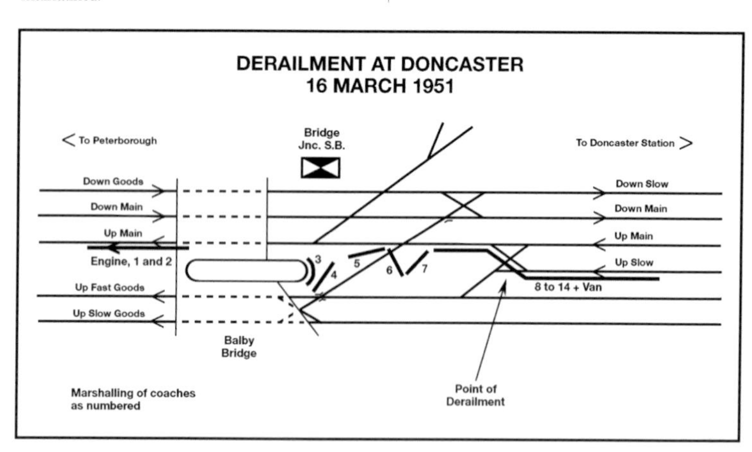

HENWICK HALL
4.45pm Monday 2 November 1964

Location: Main lines 120yd south of Henwick Hall signalbox.

The 03.17 Class 7 goods train from Millerhill to Ollerton had been checked by signals approaching Henwick Hall signalbox. It became derailed shortly after passing the signalbox, when travelling at about 20mph, and a tank wagon fouled the down main line. A down express passenger train, the 14.00 'Heart of Midlothian' from King's Cross to Edinburgh, was closely approaching at about 55mph and its driver saw the derailment occur. He made an emergency brake application and struck the tank wagon a glancing blow at about 45mph.

Cause: The goods train became divided between the 37th and 38th wagons owing to a defective coupling, and as a result of the buffering-up of the second portion, a further division occurred between the 44th and 45th wagons, the leading pair of wheels of the latter wagon being derailed towards the down main line. The derailment of the 45th wagon was caused by the condition of the springs and axleboxes. Neither the track nor the handling of the goods train was at fault.

Conditions: Dull, dry and clear. It was dusk.

Formations: *The goods train* — Type 4 diesel-electric locomotive, 52 wagons and a brakevan. Forty-four of the wagons were empty crude oil tank wagons. It had a small fitted head consisting of two empty vans and was restricted to 40mph.
The express — Type 5 diesel-electric 'Deltic' locomotive and 11 coaches. It was carrying 220 passengers.

Damage: *The goods train* — the derailed tank wagon was severely damaged and four more wagons were derailed.
The express — four coaches were derailed and all were damaged except the last three. The whole train remained upright and in line.

Casualties: Only minor injuries.

Track: Continuously welded flat-bottomed rail on concrete sleepers, except for a length of five 60ft rails on concrete sleepers and several lengths on timber sleepers just south of the signalbox where connections had been removed a fortnight earlier. The derailment occurred on the section of 60ft rails on concrete sleepers.

Possible safety measures: These were private owners' tank wagons, some of which were over 60 years old. It was recommended that tank wagons receive more frequent general overhauls and that the suitability of older wagons for use in current conditions be considered.

YORK
2.48am Saturday 11 January 1975

Location: At the points at the north end of Platform 9, at the convergence of the platform line and the down main line.

The 19.20 sleeping car express from Aberdeen to King's Cross was running alongside Platform 9 under clear signals at about 10mph prior to making its booked stop, when the last two coaches were in sidelong collision with the locomotive of the 23.15 sleeping car express from King's Cross to Aberdeen, which was passing through the station on the down main line at about 20mph.

Cause: The driver of the down (northbound) express ran past signal Y164 at danger, and the normal lie of the facing points ahead took him into sidelong collision. The layout did not permit flank protection to be given.

Conditions: Fine, with good visibility.

Formations: *The 19.20 train (1E40)* — 'Deltic' diesel-electric locomotive No 55007, 11 coaches and a guard's brakevan (BG).
The 23.15 train (1S77) — diesel-electric locomotive No 47255, three car-carrying vehicles, three coaches, six sleeping cars and a guard's brakevan (BG).

Damage: *The 19.20 train* — the BG and the last coach were derailed and damaged.
The 23.15 train — the front left-hand corner of the locomotive was crushed.

Casualties: No passengers were injured but the guard of the 19.20 was injured and detained in hospital.

Signalling: Multiple-aspect colour-light signalling with continuous track circuiting. Track circuit block regulations applied. York power signalbox controlled the whole area. Signals in the station area were not equipped with AWS owing to the complexity of routes

47425
500
Sprinter

Left: **YORK 11 January 1975**
An up express is seen arriving at Platform 9. *M.Goodfield/IAL*

and the low speeds of trains. Most lines had a 15mph speed restriction, but trains on the main lines in the right direction could travel at 25mph.

Possible safety measures: The interlocking was subsequently altered to provide approach control from red to yellow at the signal in rear of Y164 when a movement such as that of train 1E40 was taking place.

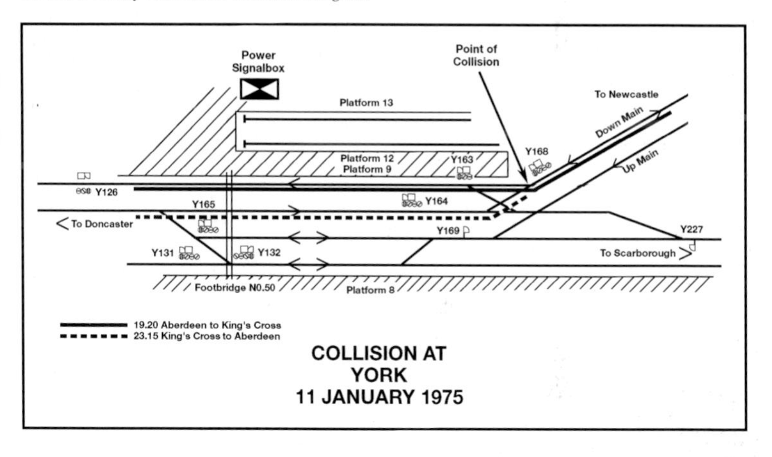

YORK
4.54pm Tuesday 15 June 1965

Location: Diamond crossings, known as Waterworks Crossing, at the north end of the station where the main lines to and from Newcastle cross the Scarborough lines to and from Platforms 14-16.

As the 15.57 passenger train from Scarborough to Leeds was proceeding over Waterworks Crossing towards Platform 15, the front vehicle was in collision with the front vehicle of the empty coaches of the 14.35 passenger train from Newcastle to York, which were being propelled at about 5mph to Clifton Carriage Sidings in the down direction along the up main line by the train engine. The passenger train had almost stopped when the collision occurred because its approach speed was low and the driver made an emergency brake application.

Cause: The empty stock train ran past colour-light signal Y165 at danger, and two position light ground signals also at danger. The traincrew of the empty stock train, driver, secondman and guard were jointly responsible. The guard of the empty stock movement was travelling in the leading coach and giving hand signals to the secondman, but he banged his head and was dazed; consequently he ceased to give hand signals. The secondman did not tell his driver that the handsignals had ceased; therefore the driver continued to propel.

Conditions: Dry and sunny.

Formations: *The passenger train* — two four-coach diesel multiple-units.
The empty stock train — five coaches being propelled by a BR/Sulzer Type 2 diesel-electric locomotive No D5149.

60073

Left: **YORK 15 June 1965**
Class A3 Pacific No 60073 *Sir Gatien* is seen passing over the famous diamond crossings at the north end of York station with a down express. The track layout has since been considerably simplified. *IAL*

Damage: *The passenger train* — the driver's compartment and the first class saloon of the leading coach were extensively damaged.
The empty stock train — the leading coach was derailed and tilted over.

Casualties: There were a number of minor injuries, but only one passenger was detained in hospital.

Signalling: Multiple-aspect colour-light signalling with continuous track circuiting. Track circuit block regulations applied. York power signalbox controlled the whole area. Signals in the station area were not equipped with AWS owing to the complexity of routes and the low speeds of trains.

Possible safety measures: It was considered that a signal should not be cleared for a propelling movement at the north end of York station until a clear road was available for the movement throughout.

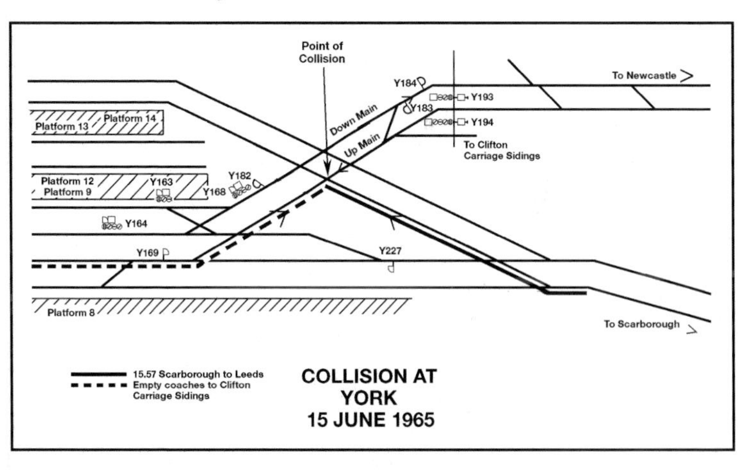

THIRSK
3.17pm Monday 31 July 1967

Location: About 2½ miles south of Thirsk. The derailment occurred at 19 miles 1,042yd from York, and the collision about 100yd further along.

A freight train, the 02.40 from Cliffe (Kent) to Uddingston, was travelling on the down slow line at about 45mph when the rear axle of the 12th wagon became derailed towards the cess. After travelling for 170yd the coupling in front broke. The 13th to 20th wagons went down the embankment, but the 23rd wagon slewed round and fouled the down main line on which the 12.00 express passenger train from King's Cross to Edinburgh was approaching at 80mph 600yd away. Its driver saw a cloud of dust ahead and applied the brakes fully, reducing speed to about 50mph when the collision occurred.

Cause: The first wagon to derail was a two-axle loaded bulk-cement wagon prone to lateral oscillation, which could lead to derailment on track having minor defects within laid down tolerances.

Formations: *The goods train* — Type 4 diesel-electric locomotive, brakevan, 26 loaded bulk-cement 'Cemflo' wagons, brakevan.
The express — Type DP2 diesel-electric locomotive and 13 coaches. The train was well filled.

Damage: The express — the locomotive and first seven coaches were derailed, and the left-hand leading corner of the locomotive was crushed. The leading coach was a corridor composite brake with the compartments on the left-hand side. The side of the coach was ripped off and the compartments were demolished. The next two coaches had their corridors on the left-hand side. The sides were badly torn. The next three coaches were damaged but not so severely.

Casualties: Seven passengers were killed and 45 were injured and detained in hospital.

The wagon: The 'Cemflo' wagons had 27-ton capacity with a tare weight of about 8½ tons and a 15ft wheelbase. They were vacuum braked. The maximum design speed was 60mph, but it was reduced to 45mph in 1965/6 following two derailments caused by broken springs. The method of suspension was found to be unsatisfactory and it was recommended that the type of buffer should be changed.

Safety measures: The maximum speed for these wagons was immediately reduced to 35mph. This was a period when there were many derailments of goods trains running at about 45mph occurring when minor irregularities in both track and wagon coincided.

NORTHALLERTON
3.50pm Tuesday 28 August 1979

Location: About ¼-mile south of Northallerton station.

As the 13.00 high-speed train from King's Cross to Edinburgh was approaching Northallerton under clear signals at a speed of about 70mph, the leading power car became derailed at a trailing crossover. The driver made an emergency brake application and the train stopped within 550yd.

Cause: The leading axle of the leading power car had seized in the York area, causing 'flats' and false flanges to be worn on the tyre. The false flange had struck the trailing crossover and damaged it, causing derailment. The seizure had been caused by gearbox failure due to lack of lubricant.

Conditions: Fine and dry.

Formation: Ten-car high-speed train set.

Damage: The whole train was derailed but remained upright.

Casualties: One passenger was detained in hospital overnight.

Possible safety measures: Improved maintenance.

DARLINGTON
11.8pm Wednesday 27 June 1928

Location: On the down main line just south of Darlington station, almost opposite the South Junction signalbox.

The 8.55pm return excursion from Scarborough to Newcastle, running at about 55mph, was about to bypass Darlington station on the outside lines, when it collided head-on with the engine of a shunting movement.

Cause: A shunting movement was being carried out by the train engine of the 9.30pm train from Newcastle to York. That train had come to a stand in the southbound platform, and required to make the following movements:

1. Draw forward to the south end of Platform 1.

Above: **NORTHALLERTON 28 August 1979**
Looking north along the derailed coaches, showing how well they remained upright and in line despite being derailed at 70mph. Northallerton signalbox can be seen behind the train. *J. M. Boyes/IAL*

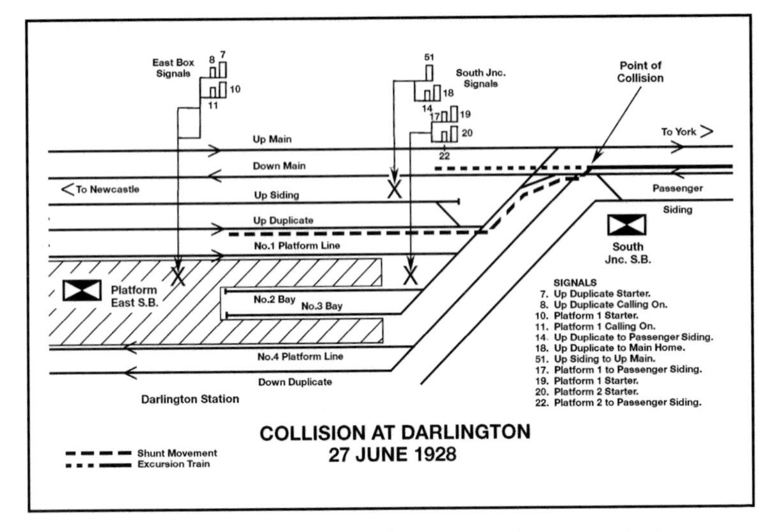

COLLISION AT DARLINGTON
27 JUNE 1928

2. Uncouple behind the third vehicle. Engine and three vehicles then to draw forward towards the passenger siding sufficiently far to clear the trailing points into the up duplicate line.

3. Engine and three vehicles set back to the north end of the up duplicate line and attach seven vehicles.

4. Draw forward to signals 14/18 and await clearance to shunt ahead towards the passenger siding sufficiently far to clear the trailing points in the up platform line.

5. Set back along the up platform line on to remainder of train previously left there.

The driver of the shunting movement when carrying out operation No 4 above wrongly passed signals 14/18 at danger and strayed on to the main line just as the excursion was approaching. He did not fully understand the signalling. He thought that the clearance of signal No 8 at Platform East signalbox authorised him to make a movement towards the south junction, and that signals 14/18 did not apply to him. The shunter in charge of the shunting movement should have stopped the movement when he saw signals 14/18 being passed at danger.

Formations: *The return excursion* — ex-NER Class Z (C7) Atlantic No 2164 with 11 vehicles.
The shunt movement — ex-NER 4-6-0 Class B16 No 2369.

Damage: The return excursion — the engine overturned, but all the coaches remained upright. However, the underframe of the third coach telescoped into the second, destroying several compartments.

Casualties: 25 passengers were killed and 45 were seriously injured. The enginemen were also seriously injured.

Signalling: Absolute block, with semaphore signals.

Possible safety measures: Improve the signalling arrangements at Platform East and South Junction signalboxes to avoid misunderstanding, and clarify the nature of the calling-on signals, which were in fact being used as shunt ahead signals.

DARLINGTON
11.49am Wednesday 11 December 1968

Location: South end of the station.

The 11.00 express passenger train from Newcastle to King's Cross failed to make its booked stop at Darlington Bank Top station, passed a signal at danger, and became derailed at the trap points at the south end of Platform 1.

Cause: Errors in the operation of the air brake equipment. The empty coaches to form the train had come from Heaton Carriage Sidings but the locomotive was changed at Newcastle Central. The secondman wrongly connected the brake pipe and the main reservoir pipe hoses on the locomotive to those on the first vehicle, connecting them respectively to the main reservoir pipe and the brake pipe. The driver and guard failed to carry out the required brake test to ensure that the braking system was in order.

Formation: Class 55 'Deltic' diesel-electric locomotive and 12 vehicles.

Damage: The locomotive and first three coaches were derailed.

Casualties: None serious.

Possible safety measures: Painting the coupling heads of the brake pipe and main reservoir pipe in different colours. The coupling heads were designed differently to prevent cross-coupling, but it was possible to do so with worn coupling heads. A redesign was required. The air brake instructions were subsequently revised.

DARLINGTON
approx 11.30am Wednesday 16 February 1977

Location: Beyond the north end of the station.

The 08.00 express passenger train from King's Cross to Edinburgh failed to make its booked station stop at Darlington and passed through the station at high speed. It passed signal D883 at danger then came into a converging collision at the north end of the station with, and derailed, the rear car of a two-car diesel multiple-unit. The express then ran on to the single track Bishop Auckland branch line from which the

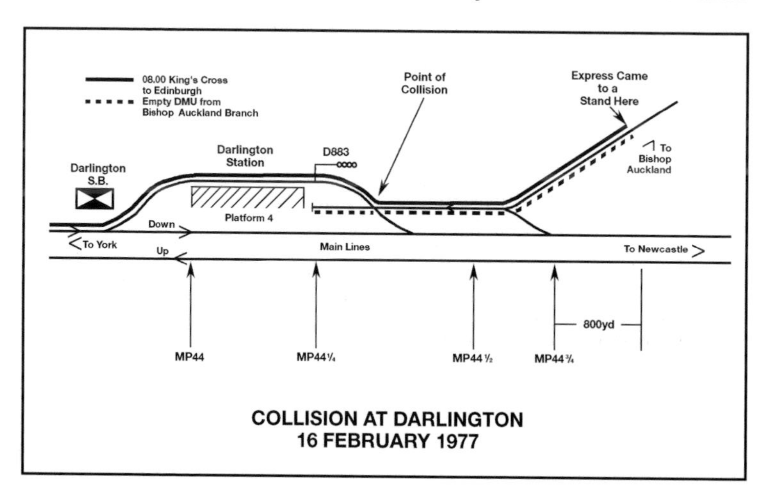

COLLISION AT DARLINGTON
16 FEBRUARY 1977

empty DMU had just come, and was brought to a stand by the operation of the passenger communication apparatus.

Cause: Failure of the airbrake. There are a number of speed restrictions at Darlington. For northbound trains there is a 35mph restriction at the south junction and a 20mph restriction along the platform line, easing to 30mph at the north end, then down to 20mph for the Bishop Auckland branch line. The train passed through the station at an estimated 55mph, retarded only by the locomotive brake. It is thought that vandals had placed a 9½in offcut of rail on the line a few miles south of Darlington and that this flew up under the train and closed the airbrake pipe cock at the front of the first coach, thus disconnecting the train's brakes from operation by the locomotive. The piece of rail was not discovered until the further incident on 3 August, described below in the postscript, and it is assumed it was responsible for both incidents. The guard should have appreciated that the train was approaching the station too fast, and applied the brake, but he said that he was thrown off his feet by a lurch of the train when attempting to do so.

Conditions: Dull and showery.

Formation: 'Deltic' diesel-electric locomotive No 55008 and 11 vehicles.

Damage: The 'Deltic' locomotive was slightly damaged but one car of the DMU was overturned. The coaches of the express were not damaged.

Casualties: None serious.

Possible safety measures: A modification of the brake pipe cock to prevent such accidental closure. This was done.

Postscript: On 3 August 1977 the 07.45 express passenger train from King's Cross to Edinburgh struck the same object at about the same location, which disconnected the brake pipes between the second and third vehicles, and between the fifth and sixth, bringing the train to a stand. The Civil Engineer was urged not to leave at the lineside such material which could be attractive to malicious people.

BETWEEN FERRYHILL AND DURHAM
5.40am Saturday 5 January 1946

Location: At Browney signalbox, just south of Milepost 63.

An up goods train had been almost stopped at Bridge House, the signalbox in rear of Browney, in order to pick up a relief signalman and when it resumed its journey the signalman at Bridge House noticed that the train had become divided between the seventh and eighth wagons. In the next two miles there were some steep falling gradients, and the signalman sent the 'Train Divided' signal to the signalman at Browney, in order to warn him. The signalman at Browney put all his signals to danger, both to stop the first portion of the divided train and to stop a down express passenger train, the 11.15pm from King's Cross to Newcastle, which was approaching.

The rear portion of the divided train soon caught up with the front portion, which was standing at Browney, and collided with it at about 25-30mph, scattering wreckage across the down main line. Some wreckage slid down the embankment and pulled the signal wires, causing the down main line signals to go to the clear position. The Newcastle express was therefore not stopped, and within 2½min it had crashed into the wreckage at about 50mph.

Cause A broken drawbar on the seventh wagon induced the division of the train.

Conditions: Dark but clear.

Formations: *The express* — Class V2 2-6-2 No 4895 and 15 vehicles.
The goods train — Class B16 4-6-0 No 842 and 44 wagons.

Damage: *The express* — the engine was turned over on to its side, and the first 10 vehicles were derailed, the second, third and fourth vehicles being wrecked.
The goods train — the engine and all the wagons in the leading portion were derailed, the wagons being thrown on to their sides. The wagons in the rear portion were piled up, except for the last 12, which remained upright.

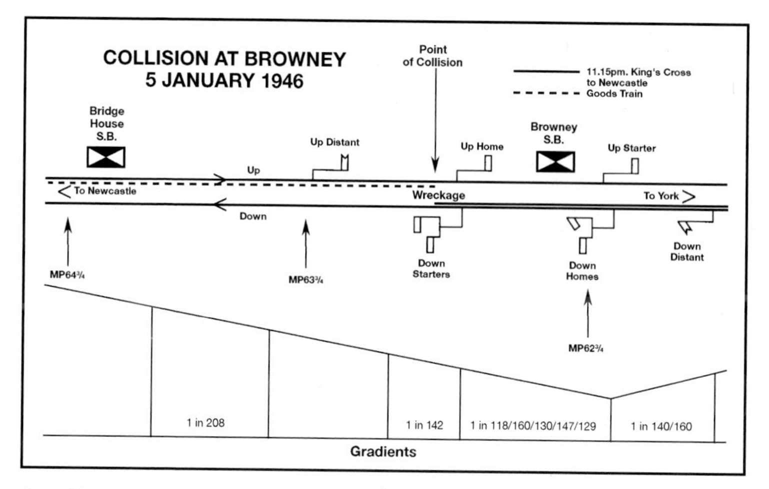

Casualties: 10 passengers were killed and 18 were injured and taken to hospital.

Signalling: Absolute block, with semaphore signals. Bridge House and Browney signalboxes were about two miles apart.

Possible safety measures: It was suggested, as it had been many times previously, that flares should be carried on trains so that early warning could be given of an obstruction on the line. Following the Dinwoodie accident on 25 October 1928 exhaustive trials were carried out by the railway companies, but it was decided that the disadvantages precluded their adoption.

It might have been more advantageous if the signalman at Browney had allowed the first portion of the divided train to proceed, as there was a rising gradient in the section ahead which would have helped to bring the rear portion to a stand.

NEAR TYNE YARD
8.59am Wednesday 1 August 1984

Location: On the down slow line at the south end of Tyne Yard, at Milepost 75¼, about five miles south of Newcastle.

As the 07.30 high-speed train (HST) from Leeds to Edinburgh was proceeding along the down slow line at about 40mph it became derailed at some trailing points. The train proceeded forward for 270yd with the last six coaches and the rear power car derailed. The train had been diverted from the down main line owing to the presence of a failed train ahead.

Cause: Faulty track at the trailing points due to inadequate maintenance.

Conditions: Fine and sunny.

Formation: Standard HST set of eight coaches and two power cars, with first class leading.

Damage: The fourth and fifth coaches slid down an embankment and turned over on to their sides.

Casualties: 25 passengers were taken to hospital, of whom three were detained with serious injuries.

Possible safety measures: A higher standard of maintenance and supervision.

MORPETH
1.31am Wednesday 7 May 1969

Location: Down main line approximately 500yd south of Morpeth station.

The 19.40 sleeping car express from King's Cross to Aberdeen, the 'Aberdonian', was derailed whilst travelling under clear signals at approximately 80mph.

Cause: The driver had failed to reduce speed for the 40mph speed-restricted curve.

Conditions: Dark and fine.

Formation: Diesel-electric 'Deltic' locomotive No D9011 and 11 vehicles, marshalled guard's brakevan, two sleeping cars, four corridor coaches, guard's brakevan, two sleeping cars, corridor coach.

Damage: The locomotive ran forward and was not derailed but the whole train was derailed. The first vehicle was destroyed, the second badly damaged, the third and fourth vehicles came to a stand in line and leaning against the cutting slope, well away from the track but badly damaged, the fifth was leaning over and badly damaged, the sixth was very badly damaged and the seventh damaged. Some coaches appeared to have been on their sides during the deceleration, but came to rest partly upright.

Casualties: Five passengers and a travelling ticket inspector were killed, and 19 passengers were seriously injured. Altogether, 121 passengers were injured, of whom 46 were detained in hospital.

Possible safety measures: It had not been the practice to give a driver advance warning of the approach to sharp curves requiring a substantial speed restriction, but subsequently illuminated advance warning signs were erected at such locations, the warning being reinforced by the provision of an AWS permanent magnet.

MORPETH
12.40am Sunday 24 June 1984

Location: Up main line, about 50yd south of the end of the platform at Morpeth station.

Shortly after the 19.50 sleeping car express from Aberdeen to King's Cross had passed through Morpeth station under clear signals at about 85-90mph it became derailed on the sharp curve.

Cause: The driver failed to reduce speed for the permanent speed restriction of 50mph.

Conditions: Dark, but clear.

Formation: Diesel-electric locomotive No 47452 and nine vehicles, marshalled guard's brakevan, seven sleeping cars and a guard's brakevan.

Damage: The entire train was derailed. The locomotive came to rest leaning against a bank and the first two vehicles turned over on to their sides and jack-knifed across both lines. The remainder of the train broke loose and went off at a tangent. All except the last two vehicles turned over on to their sides. There was remarkably little internal damage.

Casualties: 35 injured people were taken to hospital, but only three were detained — the driver and two sleeping car attendants.

Possible safety measures: There was no advance warning indicator on the up line for the sharp curve, as it was approached by a cascade of descending speed restrictions (80mph, 70mph and 50mph) and did not qualify for one under the specifications which applied at the time. They were subsequently amended to close this loophole. Automatic Train Protection would have prevented this accident.

The driver had consumed some alcohol before taking charge of the locomotive at Edinburgh and was tried at Newcastle Crown Court with endangering the lives of passengers. He was found not guilty.

Postscript: There was a further high-speed derailment on the Morpeth curve on 27 June 1994, when the locomotive and seven vans of a Rail Express Systems train, the 16.33 from King's Cross to

Glasgow, left the rails. The driver was injured. Although the curve was protected by an advance warning indicator and associated AWS permanent magnet, it was ineffective. Automatic Train Protection would have prevented this accident.

Above: **MORPETH 24 June 1984**
The derailed locomotive is seen lying on its side. *I. S. Carr*

Below: **MORPETH 24 June 1984**
Looking southwards from Morpeth station, showing the severity of the curve. A derailed coach demolished the gable end of the house in the centre of the photograph. *Author*

CHEVINGTON
5.43am Saturday 13 September 1913

Location: Down main line at Felton Lane level crossing, ¼-mile south of Chevington station.

The 11.45pm express passenger train from King's Cross to Edinburgh was completely derailed when travelling at 55-60mph under clear signals.

Cause: Defective track. The track had not been fully ballasted after permanent way operations.

Formation: An Atlantic 4-4-2 passenger engine and six vehicles, marshalled six-wheeled van, one 12-wheeled and one eight-wheeled coach, a 12-wheeled sleeping car, one 12-wheeled and one eight-wheeled coach. The train conveyed only 21 passengers.

Damage: The whole train was derailed but none of the coaches was overturned. Damage was mainly external.

Casualties: There were no serious injuries.

Possible safety measures: A temporary speed restriction should be imposed until the track is fit for normal speeds.

BETWEEN ACKLINGTON AND CHEVINGTON
6.58pm Saturday 15 July 1967

Location: Up main line, 1¾ miles north of Chevington signalbox (23¼ miles north of Newcastle).

The up 'North Briton' express passenger train from Edinburgh to Leeds was travelling at about 75mph under clear signals, when it became derailed.

Cause: Broken rail-end.

Conditions: Fine.

Formation: Type 4 BR/Sulzer diesel-electric locomotive and 12 vehicles. The train conveyed 160 passengers.

Damage: The locomotive was partly derailed, but all the coaches left the rails. However, they remained mostly upright and fairly well in line.

Casualties: Only nine passengers required hospital treatment. They were ferried to the ambulances by helicopters from the nearby RAF station at Acklington.

Track: The rails were 95lb bull-head laid in 1941, in cast-iron chairs on wooden sleepers. There was only one fishbolt hole at each end. This length of track was programmed for renewal in October 1967.

Left: **BETWEEN ACKLINGTON AND CHEVINGTON 15 July 1967**
Looking southwards along the derailed train, showing the extent of damage to the track. A rescue helicopter can just be seen hovering over the front of the train.
Author's Collection

Signalling: Colour-light signals and continuous track circuiting were provided. The area was controlled from Chevington signalbox.

Possible safety measures: The former-LNER single fishbolt arrangement had not been a success, and it was decided that the few remaining miles of such track should be converted to the normal two fishbolt holes. In the meantime, rail-ends with single fishbolt holes were to have more frequent inspection.

BETWEEN CHATHILL AND BELFORD
12.35pm Sunday 28 May 1972

Location: Up main line approx ¾-mile north of Chathill signalbox.

The 11.00 express passenger train from Edinburgh to King's Cross was travelling at about 80mph under clear signals, when the leading coach was derailed.

Cause: Both fishplates in a bolted joint were broken.

Conditions: Cool and showery.

Formation: 'Deltic' diesel-electric locomotive and 12 vehicles.

Damage: All 12 vehicles were derailed, but remained coupled, almost upright, and in line.

Casualties: Only a few minor injuries.

The track: 60ft 109lb flat-bottomed rails laid in 1949 on wooden sleepers. At the point of derailment there was an 11ft 10in closure rail, the end of which had been flame-cut. Wear and tear formed a chisel-edge on the end, which initiated fatigue cracks at the top of each fishplate. The track was near the end of its life and in poor condition, and was booked to be relaid in 1973. It is of interest that in 1964 the future of the line north of Newcastle was in doubt and all track renewals were deferred. It was proposed to single the line from Alnmouth to Dunbar. However, in 1967 the plan was changed and it was then proposed to lay continuous welded rail on both lines as far as the regional boundary north of Berwick. This work was still in progress when the derailment occurred.

Possible safety measures: Closer inspection of track, and better supervision.

GOSWICK
12.33am Wednesday 28 August 1907

Location: Up main/up independent facing points.

The 11.22pm up braked goods from Tweedmouth to Newcastle was derailed whilst entering the connection to the up independent at 55-60mph.

Cause: The train was travelling too fast. The turnout was suitable for only a low rate of speed, and another driver said that he would go through it at only 5mph. The train was being diverted to the up independent line so that the 11.15pm express from Edinburgh to King's Cross could pass it. The signalman at Goswick signalbox set his points towards the independent line after he had accepted the train, but failed to bring the train almost to a stand at his outermost stop signal, as required by Rule 40, because his following stop signals were still at danger. The premature clearance of this signal might have misled the driver into believing that the up main home and up starting signals were also clear for the main line (which they were not), and he ran past them at danger at high speed.

Formation: NER 4-6-0 No 2005 and 20 braked vehicles.

Damage: The engine was derailed and turned over, landing on its side in a ditch. Most of the wagons were destroyed or damaged.

Casualties: The driver and fireman were killed.

Signalling: Absolute block with semaphore signals. The block sections were Scremerston-Goswick and Goswick-Beal.

Possible safety measures: Strict application of Rule 40.

Above: **GOSWICK 28 August 1907**
The derailed engine lies upside down in a ditch. *C. R. L. Coles Collection/IAL*

GOSWICK
12.47pm Sunday 26 October 1947

Location: Up main/up independent facing points at Goswick, about seven miles south of Berwick.

The up main line beyond Goswick was blocked by engineering work, and it was necessary to divert trains to the up independent line, requiring a reduction of speed to 15-20mph. The 11.15am express passenger train from Edinburgh to King's Cross was derailed whilst traversing the facing connection from the main line to the independent line at about 50mph.

Cause: The driver failed to reduce speed to the required level. He also failed to observe and obey the distant signal at caution and failed to slow down for the home signal, which was cleared as he approached it. He passed the starting signal at danger. There was some conflict of evidence between the driver and the signalman about the working of the home and starting signals. The driver thought that the starting signal had been cleared, but the signalman said that it had not, and that he did not clear it because he saw the train approaching at high speed.

Conditions: Bright and clear.

Formation: Class A3 Pacific No 60066 *Merry Hampton* and 15 bogie vehicles. The train conveyed approximately 420 passengers.

Damage: The engine and eight of the first nine vehicles went down a low bank into a ditch. The fourth coach, which was the leading coach of a triple articulated set, broke away and came to rest across the up line. The last six remained upright and in line, the last four being not derailed. Six coaches were wrecked and four badly damaged.

Casualties: 27 passengers and a train attendant were killed. The driver and fireman were seriously injured, and 59 passengers and six railway staff were detained in hospital.

Signalling: Absolute block with semaphore signals. The distant signal was 1,647yd from the home signal.

Possible safety measures: AWS would have avoided this accident. It was subsequently decided that Rule 39(a) should apply to unbooked movements over low speed junctions, so that the home signal would not be cleared until the signalman was satisfied that the train had come quite or nearly to a stand at it.

Above: **GOSWICK 26 October 1947**
An aerial view of the crash site, showing the considerable extent of destruction of the train. *NRM*

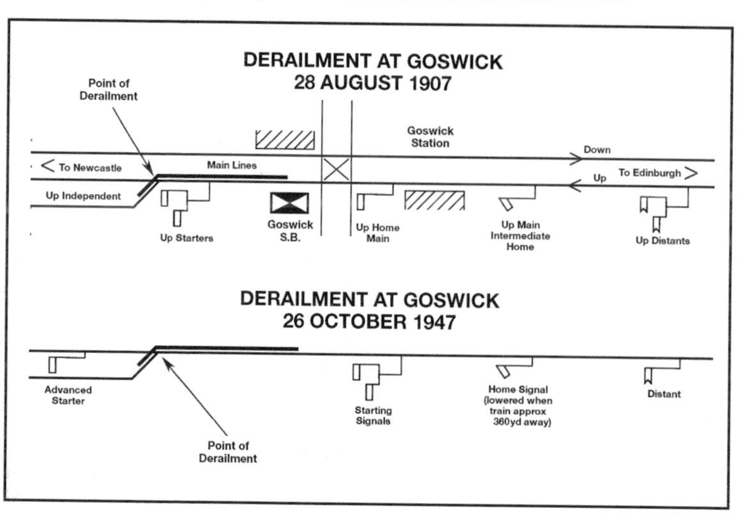

PENMANSHIEL TUNNEL, BETWEEN COCKBURNSPATH AND GRANTSHOUSE
8.40pm Thursday 23 June 1949

Location: Up main line, about 3¼ miles south of Cockburnspath.

Fire broke out in the tenth coach of the 7.30pm express passenger train from Edinburgh to King's Cross whilst it was travelling at about 25mph, and the train was brought to a stand partly inside the entrance to the tunnel, the last three vehicles being still outside the tunnel.

Cause: Probably a lighted match or a cigarette end thrown carelessly against the foot of the wall in the leading transverse corridor of the coach, a corridor brake composite, which quickly ignited the wooden partition because it had been sprayed with clear cellulose lacquer. The fire spread very rapidly, but fortunately the guard was riding in that coach and stopped the train quickly. The train was uncoupled behind the eighth coach, and the front portion was drawn forward.

Conditions: Fine, dry and warm.

Formation: Class A3 Pacific No 60035 *Windsor Lad* and 12 vehicles, marshalled mail van, four coaches, guard's brakevan, sleeping car, three corridor coaches, buffet car, guard's brakevan. The train conveyed 170 passengers.

Damage: Two coaches, the ninth and tenth, were completely gutted.

Casualties: Seven passengers were injured, two seriously.

The coach: A corridor brake composite, of steel and wood construction, built in 1947. Marshalled with first class compartments and guard's compartment at the rear.

Possible safety measures: The use of cellulose lacquer as a finish was abandoned, and it was removed from existing coaches.

DREM
10.28pm Saturday 25 March 1972

Location: Up main line at the west end of Drem station, near Milepost 17¾.

A goods train was being shunted back into a refuge siding for an express passenger train to pass, but it was found that the train was too long to be accommodated in the siding, and the two locomotives of the train were still foul of the main line when the express collided with them at about 15mph.

Cause: The driver of the express passenger train had passed the outer home signal at danger and had mishandled the vacuum brake. He was inexperienced in driving the type of locomotive being used on the express, but the rostered driver was riding in the rear cab.

Conditions: Dark, with good visibility.

Formation: *The 22.10 from Edinburgh to King's Cross* — Class 40 diesel-electric locomotive No 280 and nine vehicles. The train conveyed about 100 passengers.
The goods train — an engineer's train conveying prefabricated track and tracklaying gantries, hauled by diesel-electric locomotives Nos 263 (Class 40) leading, and 6846 (Class 37).

Damage: All three locomotives, and the leading coach (a guard's brakevan) were damaged. The locomotive of the express was completely derailed.

Casualties: None.

Signalling: Absolute block. The up main colour-light distant signal was 1,589yd from the up outer home signal, the latter being approx 460yd from the fouling point with the refuge siding. There was no inner home signal. The distant signal was equipped with AWS. The line speed was 80mph.

Possible safety measures: Automatic Train Protection would prevent accidents of this nature. The rostered driver should travel in the front cab in order to supervise.

PRESTONPANS
Thursday 22 May 1980

Location: Up main line approaching Prestonpans.

A sleeping car express from Edinburgh to King's Cross was approaching Prestonpans at almost 70mph when nearly all the train was derailed.

Cause: A vandal had placed on the track a piece of rail nearly 6ft long and weighing about 2cwt. The culprit, a 17-year-old youth, was apprehended and committed to Borstal.

Above: **PRESTONPANS 22 May 1980**
Looking southwards along the derailed train, which remained upright and generally in line. *I. M. Flynn*

Formation: Locomotive, two vehicles, six sleeping cars and a guard's brakevan.

Damage: All the coaches after the second one were derailed, but remained in line.

Casualties: No serious injuries.

Possible safety measures: Material that might attract vandals should not be left at the lineside.

HAYMARKET
6.58pm Monday 28 July 1924

Location: Down south platform at Haymarket station.

The 6.41pm Inner Circle passenger train was standing in Haymarket station when it was run into in the rear at about 10mph by the 6.54pm local passenger train from Edinburgh to Kirkliston.

Cause: There was conflicting evidence, but it appears that the driver of the 6.54pm train ran past the starting signal at danger at Princes Street Gardens signalbox, although the signalman did not maintain his home signal at danger until the train was close to it, as required by the rules. Had he done so, the driver should have been alerted to the fact of the starting signal being at danger.

Formations: *The 6.41pm train* — Class C15 4-4-2T No 133 and nine coaches, including eight four-wheelers.

The 6.54pm train — Class D29 4-4-0 No 9338, with three eight-wheeled coaches and a brakevan.

Damage: *The 6.41pm train* — the second coach from the rear telescoped into the vehicle ahead, crushing several compartments. The last three coaches were practically destroyed.
The 6.54pm train — minor.

Casualties: Five passengers were killed and 54 were injured.

Signalling: The lock and block system was in use, with absolute block. There were no detonator placing machines at Princes Street Gardens signalbox.

Possible safety measures: Strict application of Rule 40(a), that when a starting signal is at danger, the stop signal next in rear should not be taken off until the train is close to it and has been brought quite or nearly to a stand.

POLMONT EAST
7.20am Monday 5 February 1962

Location: Down main line just east of Polmont East signalbox, 93yd beyond the outer home signal.

The 5.25am Class C goods train had been stopped at Polmont East outer home signal, and was just drawing ahead at 15-20mph when it was run into in the rear by the 6.50am express passenger train from Edinburgh to Callander, which was running under clear signals at 35-40mph. Its speed had been reduced from 50-55mph when the driver saw the freight train ahead. The passenger train was booked to stop at Polmont station.

Cause: Serious block signalling irregularities. The berth track circuit at Polmont East outer home signal had failed, locking the block instruments, and to overcome the problem the signalmen had been irregularly manipulating the track proving relay in such a way as to unlock the block instruments and eliminate the block controls. The signalman had forgotten about the goods train which was standing at his outer home signal, and it did not register its presence on his illuminated diagram. When he wrongly accepted the passenger train from Bo'ness Junction signalbox he cleared all his signals for it, and the goods train driver, having seen the outer home signal move to the clear position, started to draw forward.

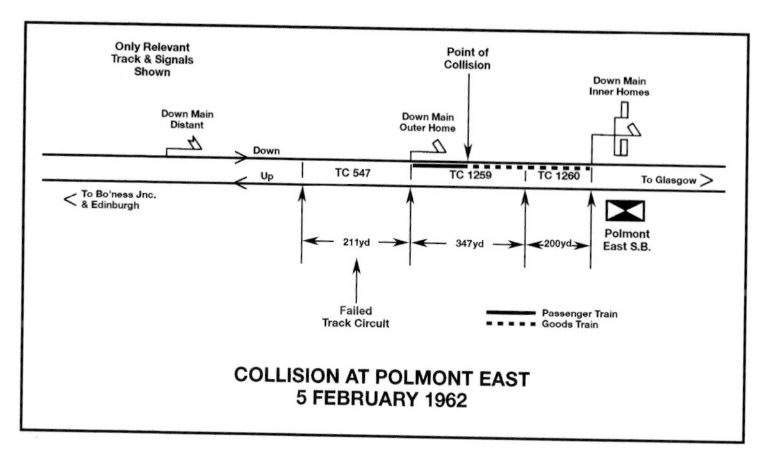

COLLISION AT POLMONT EAST
5 FEBRUARY 1962

Conditions: Clear, cold, dawn breaking.

Formation: *The passenger train* — ex-LMS 2-6-4T and five coaches.
The goods train — ex-LNER Class V2 2-6-2, 18 wagons and brakevan, fully-fitted.

Damage: *The passenger train* — the engine and the first coach were derailed but not badly damaged.
The goods train — three wagons and the brakevan were derailed, the brakevan and last wagon being wrecked.

Casualties: There were no serious injuries, but a small number of minor ones.

Signalling: Absolute block with semaphore signals. AWS was provided at the distant signals.

Possible safety measures: Better supervision. Relay cupboards to be kept locked and the keys retained by the technician.

BETWEEN POLMONT AND FALKIRK
5.55pm Monday 30 July 1984

Location: Down main line, about 200yd beyond Milepost 23¾.

The 17.30 express passenger train from Edinburgh to Glasgow was travelling at about 85mph under clear signals, when it hit an obstruction and became derailed. A similar train approaching in the opposite direction managed to stop about 200yd clear when its driver saw a coach somersaulting.

Cause: A fully-grown cow weighing about 8cwt had gained access to the line and was struck by the train, becoming lodged under the front of the first vehicle. It was thought that the cow had gained access to the line at a point where the fencing had been damaged by trespassers.

Weather: Clear.

Formation: Class 47/7 diesel-electric locomotive No 47707 propelling five Mk 3 coaches, with a Mk 2 DBSO (driving brake second open) leading.

Damage: The DBSO became derailed and ran up a cutting slope, turning almost end to end and coming to rest on its side, badly damaged. The second coach was turned end to end and came to rest across the up line, still upright. The remainder of the train was derailed and suffered some damage, but remained upright and in line.

Casualties: 13 passengers were killed and 14 were seriously injured. Three railway staff were also seriously injured. Many were slightly injured.

The lineside fencing: A mixture of four-strand and seven-strand post and wire fencing and stone walls.

Possible safety measures: Large animals to be treated as a potential obstruction, and drivers to be warned. Trains to be equipped with radio, so that emergency warnings can be given, both by drivers to signalmen and from signalmen to drivers. Improved maintenance of fencing. Fitting of deflectors to leading vehicles. Increase the axle-load of DBSOs.

CASTLECARY
4.37pm Friday 10 December 1937

Location: Down main line at Castlecary station, in rear of the down starting signal.

The 2pm express passenger train from Dundee to Glasgow ran past the home signal at danger at Castlecary, but the signalman realised that it was going to do so and he used his handlamp to show a red light to the driver as the train went past the signalbox. The signalman did not know whether the driver had seen the red light or not, but he had done so and had stopped his train more or less at the starting signal. The signalman did not see that the train had stopped, although he should have done, because he could have seen the tail lamp from the signalbox, and he ought to have seen that his track circuit indicator for that section of line was showing 'occupied'. The signalman wrongly gave 'Train out of Section' to the signalbox in rear (he did not have the required ¼-mile clearance inside the home signal) and he wrongly accepted the following train, the 4.3pm express passenger train from Edinburgh to Glasgow. This train also ran past the home signal at danger and crashed into the standing Dundee train at about 60mph.

Cause: There was conflicting evidence — both the driver of the train from Dundee and the driver of the train from Edinburgh maintained that the distant signal was clear, but the signalman could not have pulled the distant signal lever as the Dundee train was standing on his track circuit and the interlocking would have prevented him from doing so. It is possible that the arm of the distant signal had drooped, owing to slackness in the wire or the weight of snow on the arm. The driver of the Edinburgh train was charged with culpable homicide in the

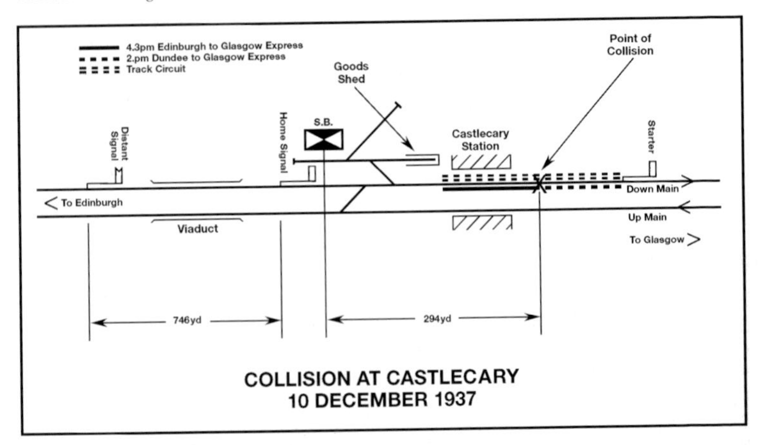

Right: **CASTLECARY 10 December 1937**
Clearing-up operations, showing how one of the coaches somersaulted over the tender on to the engine, which lies buried in a pile of wreckage. ***Hulton-Deutsch***

Edinburgh High Court on 30 March 1938, but the next day the Lord Advocate withdrew the charge and directed the jury to return a verdict of not guilty. The signalman was seriously at fault for (1) giving 'Train out of Section' whilst the Dundee train was still within his ¼-mile clearance, (2) for accepting the Edinburgh train without having the ¼-mile clearance, (3) failing to observe the Dundee train standing in rear of his starting signal, either visually or by observance of his track circuit indicator, (4) failing to ensure that the distant signal arm was horizontal, by observance of the backlight.

Conditions: Dark, with heavy snow showers.

Formations: *The Dundee train* — ex-NBR Class D29 'Scott' 4-4-0 No 9896 *Dandie Dinmont*, seven bogie coaches and a six-wheeled fishvan. The train conveyed 110 passengers.
The Edinburgh train — Class A3 Pacific No 2744 *Grand Parade* and nine bogie coaches, including a restaurant car. The train conveyed almost 200 passengers and six dining car staff.

Damage: *The Dundee train* — the fishvan and the last two coaches, a brake third and a composite coach, were demolished.
The Edinburgh train — the engine was overturned and the first three coaches (two third class and a brake third) were projected over the top of it, being very severely damaged.

Casualties: 22 passengers were killed in the Dundee train and 13 in the Edinburgh train. A total of 179 passengers were injured, many seriously. At the time, it was the worst ever peacetime collision in Britain, in terms of fatalities.

Signalling: Absolute block with semaphore signals. The position of the down distant signal arm was not repeated in the signalbox, nor was it interlinked with the block instrument.

Possible safety measures: Provide a repeater for the distant signal arm, and interlink it with the block instruments to prevent 'Line Clear' being given to the signalbox in rear unless the distant signal arm was proved to be in the caution position. This equipment had already been installed at 31% of the distant signals on the Edinburgh-Glasgow line. AWS would have prevented this accident if the arm had been in the caution position.

CASTLECARY STATION (CLOSED)
9.15am Monday 9 September 1968

Location: Up main line near signal GU5B, on the Glasgow side of the old station. Near Milepost 15½.

The 08.46 passenger train from Glasgow to Edinburgh was standing at signal GU5B when it was run into in the rear by a diesel-electric locomotive running light at about 35-40mph.

Cause: A track circuit failure had held a signal at danger and drivers were being authorised by the signalman at Greenhill Upper Junction, by telephone, to go past it. He failed to instruct drivers to proceed cautiously, as required by the rules. There was some confusion in the passing of messages from the signalman, resulting in messages being received by the wrong drivers, but the main cause was the failure of the driver of the light locomotive to proceed at a sufficiently low speed that would have enabled him to stop safely, short of the train ahead, as required by the rules.

Conditions: Overcast, but reasonable visibility.

Formation: A six-car diesel multiple-unit

Damage: Minor derailment. The locomotive cab was crushed, and fire broke out, gutting the rear coach of the multiple-unit.

Casualties: The driver and secondman of the light locomotive were killed. There were a few minor injuries.

Signalling: Track circuit block between Dullatur and Greenhill Upper Junction, with multiple-aspect colour-light signalling.

Possible safety measures: Strict adherence to the procedures for passing messages by telephone. Drivers to proceed cautiously after passing a signal at danger, and to be ready to stop clear of any obstruction.

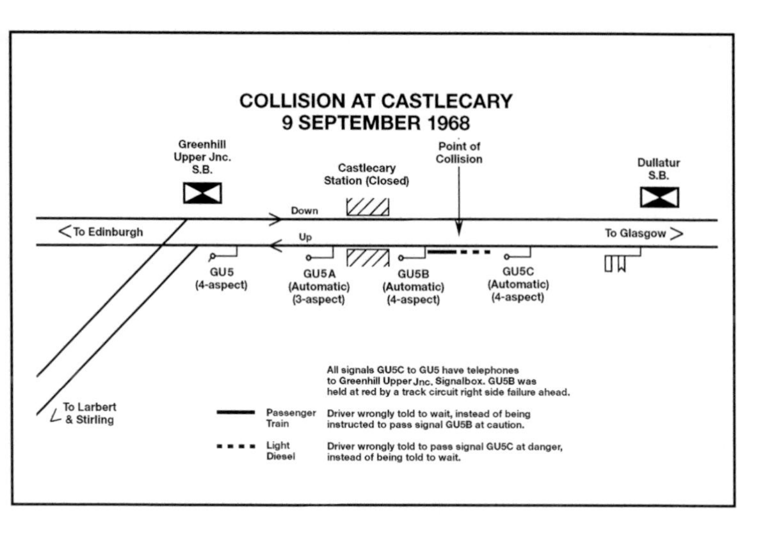

CADDER
Tuesday 16 August 1983

Location: Down main line at Cadder signalbox, about 5½ miles from Glasgow.

The 18.30 express passenger train from Edinburgh to Glasgow caught fire and was stopped by signals opposite the signalbox by the signalman replacing his signals to danger.

Cause: The fire began in a foam-type gangway unit between the fourth and fifth coaches, and was probably started by a carelessly discarded cigarette end.

Conditions: Sunny and warm.

Formation: A push-pull set, with DBSO (driver brake second open) leading, followed by four open coaches and the locomotive, a Class 47 diesel-electric.

Damage: The interiors of both coaches were severely damaged for about half their length.

Casualties: None serious.

Possible safety measures: The foam-type gangway units were already being replaced and most coaches had already been dealt with.

COWLAIRS
4.56pm Friday 30 January 1942

Location: Down main line, opposite Cowlairs East signalbox.

The 4pm express passenger train from Edinburgh to Glasgow, running under clear signals at about 35mph, collided with a stationary light engine.

Cause: The signalman had allowed a light engine to come from the adjacent Eastfield engine shed to stand on the down main line to await a path on the up main line, but he had then forgotten that it was there and had cleared his signals along the down main line for the express. The light engine had been

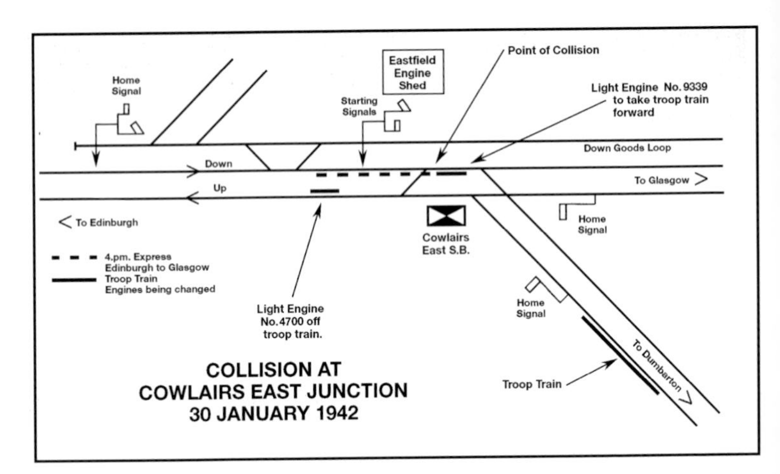

standing for only 2-3min, giving little time for the fireman of the light engine to go to the signalbox to remind the signalman of the presence of the engine, as required by Rule 55.

Conditions: Daylight and clear visibility.

Formations: *The passenger train* —Class D11 'Director' 4-4-0 No 6401 *James Fitzjames* and nine bogie vehicles.

The light engine — ex-NBR Class D29 'Scott' 4-4-0 No 9339 *Ivanhoe*.

Damage: Both engines were severely damaged and the first two coaches were partly destroyed.

Casualties: 12 passengers and the two drivers were killed, and 10 passengers were detained in hospital.

Possible safety measures: Provide track circuits.

GLASGOW QUEEN STREET STATION
5.7am Saturday 24 December 1977

Location: Platform 5.

A diesel locomotive, running light under clear signals from Cowlairs to Queen Street, got out of control on the falling gradients (1 in 45 in Queen Street Tunnel) and entered the station at 40-45mph. It crashed into the coaches of the Euston to Mallaig train, due to depart Queen Street at 6am.

Cause: Faulty brakes, caused by inadequate maintenance. The brakes had not been properly adjusted, nor packing pieces fitted.

Conditions: Dry and clear.

Formation: *The 06.00 to Mallaig* — five vehicles, including sleeping cars.
The light diesel-electric locomotive — Class 40, No 40164.

Damage: The rearmost vehicle, a sleeping car, was extensively damaged. There was some internal damage in other sleeping cars and coaches.

Casualties: There were no serious injuries.

Possible safety measures: Improved maintenance and supervision.

3 — GREAT WESTERN MAIN LINE

PADDINGTON TO PENZANCE VIA BRISTOL

APPROACHING PADDINGTON STATION
6.11am Wednesday 23 November 1983

Location: Facing points in the up main line to Platforms 7-13, near Ranelagh Bridge.

The 21.35 sleeping car express from Penzance to Paddington became derailed at the immediate approaches to the station.

Cause: Excessive speed. The train was travelling in excess of 65mph through facing points with a maximum permitted speed of 25mph. It was concluded that the driver had lost his concentration and failed to apply the brake, but he maintained that the brakes had failed.

Conditions: Dark but clear, with good visibility.

Formation: Class 50 diesel-electric locomotive No 50041 and 14 vehicles, marshalled two guards' brakevans and a sleeping car, attached at Plymouth, and a guard's brakevan, three sleeping cars, two coaches, a guard's brakevan, three coaches, and a bogie van. Air braked.

Damage: The locomotive came to rest on its side, whilst the first 12 vehicles were completely derailed, leaning over at various angles.

Signalling: Multiple-aspect colour-light signalling with continuous track circuiting. AWS equipment is provided at signals.

Casualties: Three passengers had minor injuries.

Possible safety measures: Advance warning signs of the speed restriction, with AWS, might have prevented the accident. ATP might also have prevented it.

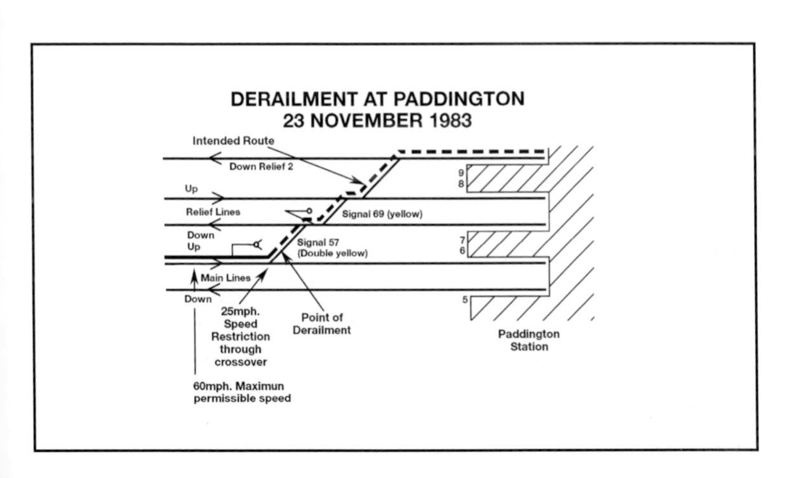

ROYAL OAK STATION
16.20 Friday 10 November 1995

Location: On the approaches to Paddington station, on adjoining parallel lines.

The 13.32 high-speed train (HST) from Swansea was approaching Paddington station when it was in sidelong collision with a Thames-Turbo empty stock train.

Cause: The driver of the empty stock train apparently misread the new signalling in the area, and thought that the yellow aspect displayed by signal SN72 was intended for him, whereas it was in actual fact cleared for the high-speed train (HST) approaching on Line 2. He ran past his own signal (SN74) at danger, into collision.

Formations: *The HST* — a standard HST set.
The Thames-Turbo train — two Class 165 diesel multiple-units (one three-car and one two-car).

Damage: *The HST* — the leading power car, and one bogie of the next coach, were derailed. The train conveyed about 250 passengers.
The Thames-Turbo train — the third and fourth coaches were turned over on to their sides.

Casualties: The HST driver was seriously injured, and 12 passengers were slightly injured.

Possible safety measures: Automatic train protection or similar apparatus, to check that the driver is obeying a restrictive signal.

WEST EALING
Approx 5.40pm Wednesday 19 December 1973

Location: Half a mile beyond Ealing Broadway station, on the down fast line.

The 17.18 outer suburban passenger train from Paddington to Oxford was derailed whilst travelling at about 70mph under clear signals.

Cause: A battery box cover at the side of the locomotive fell open and struck some point rodding, which caused a set of facing points to move as the locomotive was passing over them. The battery box doors had not been properly secured after the locomotive had received repairs and maintenance at Old Oak Common depot.

Formation: 'Western' class diesel-hydraulic locomotive No 1007 *Western Talisman* and 11 Mk 1 side-corridor coaches. The train conveyed approx 650 passengers.

Damage: The locomotive was derailed and overturned. The first coach was derailed, but the next five coaches jack-knifed and were badly damaged, the ends being crushed. All the remaining coaches were derailed.

Casualties: 10 passengers were killed and 53 injured passengers were taken to hospital.

Possible safety measures: Improved means of securing battery box lids, and improved supervision.

SOUTHALL
1.14pm Friday 19 September 1997

Location: Up main line, at a ladder of crossovers.

The 10.32 high-speed train (HST) from Swansea to Paddington collided with a train of empty hoppers which was crossing the up main line from the relief lines via the ladder of crossovers.

Cause: To be established. A public inquiry has been announced by the Government.

Formations: *The HST* — a standard HST set of seven coaches with the first class section leading. *The freight train* — empty stone hopper wagons.

Damage: *The HST* — the leading power car was derailed but remained upright. The first coach was thrown to the left and landed on its side. The second coach was badly damaged and crushed against one of the wagons. The third and fourth coaches were damaged at the ends but remained upright, whilst the remainder of the train escaped serious damage.

Casualties: Seven passengers were killed and 13 were seriously injured. The deaths occurred in the second coach. This was the first occasion that a passenger in an HST had been killed in a collision since the trains were introduced in 1976.

Signalling: Modern signalling with multiple-aspect colour-light signalling and continuous track-circuiting. The line and the train were equipped with AWS. The Automatic Train Protection system was also on extended trial on this line.

Possible safety measures: These will depend on the findings of the inquiry.

LANGLEY
9.21pm Monday 1 March 1937

Location: Trap points at the end of the up goods loop, west of Langley station.

The 7.45pm empty spoil train from Reading West Junction to Old Oak Common, running along the up goods loop at 12-15mph, passed the home signal at danger and was derailed at the facing trap points, which were set away from the main line. The engine was thrown clear, but four wagons were derailed, two of which came to rest across the up relief line on which the 6.35pm passenger train from Oxford to Paddington was closely approaching. The passenger train was running under clear signals but was slowing down for the Langley stop when it hit the derailed wagons at a speed of 20-25mph.

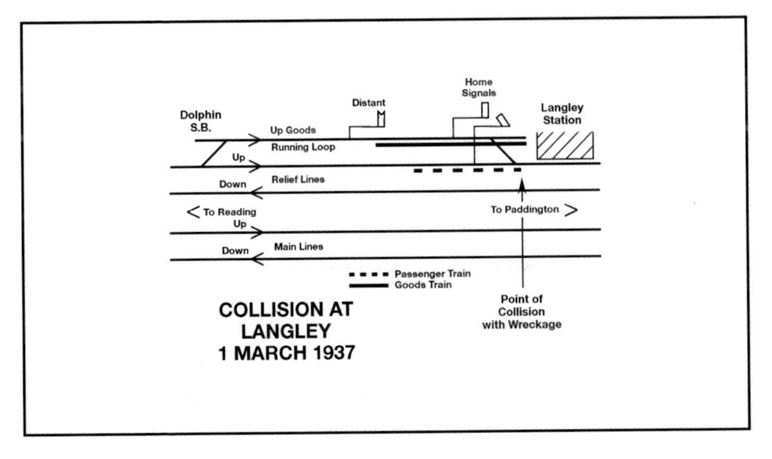

Cause: The driver of the goods train did not see the distant signal, but then his attention wandered and at the last minute he glanced up at the home signals and mistook the up relief line home signal (which was clear for the passenger train) for his own. Both the relief line signal and the goods loop signal were on separate posts to the left of the goods loop.

Conditions: Clear, but dark.

Formation: *The passenger train* — 2-6-2T No 6167, four bogie coaches and a six-wheeled milk truck.
The goods train — 2-6-0 No 6320, 25 steel ballast wagons and a brakevan.

Damage: *The passenger train* — the engine was damaged and derailed, and three coaches were derailed.
The goods train — the engine ran off the end of the rails and was damaged. Four wagons were derailed.

Casualties: The guard of the passenger train was killed.

Track and signalling: The up goods loop extended one mile from Dolphin to Langley and had a maximum permitted speed of 10mph. The signalling was absolute block with semaphore signals.

Possible safety measures: Extend the goods loop trap points into a sand drag. Reposition the up relief line home signal post between the relief line and the goods loop. The GWR adopted both these measures.

BETWEEN LANGLEY AND SLOUGH
2.55am Wednesday 2 July 1941

Location: Down relief line at the diamond crossing of the crossover from the up main line to the up relief line, at Dolphin signalbox. Approx one mile east of Slough.

The 6.20pm express passenger train from Plymouth to Paddington had just restarted after being brought to a stand at Dolphin signalbox, and was crossing from the up main line to the up relief line when it collided, engine to engine, with the 1.30am goods train from Old Oak Common to Severn Tunnel Junction.

Cause: The Inspecting Officer who inquired into this accident concluded that the signalman had cleared his signals for the goods train to run straight along the down relief line, but had then decided to run the express first, diverting it from the up main line to the up relief line across the path of the goods train. The signalman replaced to danger his down

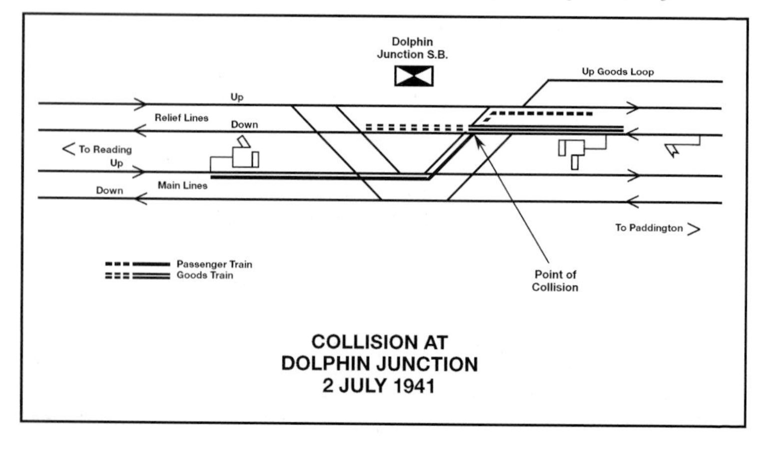

COLLISION AT DOLPHIN JUNCTION 2 JULY 1941

relief line signals in order to set his points for the diversion of the express, but by this time it is probable that the goods train had already passed the distant signal in the clear position. When the driver of the goods train saw the home signal at danger he was too close to it to be able to stop clear of the junction.

Conditions: Dark and clear.

Formations: *The express* — 'Castle' class 4-6-0 No 4091 *Dudley Castle* and eight bogie vehicles.
The goods train — LMSR 2-8-0 engine No 8293 (on loan to the GWR), 62 wagons and brakevan.

Damage: *The express* — the two leading coaches telescoped.
The goods train — several wagons piled up in a heap behind the tender.

Casualties: Five passengers were killed and five were seriously injured. The goods engine driver was also seriously injured.

Signalling: Absolute block, with semaphore signals. Automatic train control at the distant signals. The goods engine was not fitted with ATC apparatus, but it was irrelevant in the circumstances of this accident.

Possible safety measures: Improve the sighting of the down relief line home signal. Signalmen to work strictly to the regulations.

SLOUGH STATION
Saturday 16 June 1900

Location: Down main line at Slough station.

The 1.5pm passenger train from Paddington was standing in Slough station, when it was run into in the rear at about 25-30mph by the 1.15pm express passenger train from Paddington to Falmouth.

Cause: The driver of the Falmouth express had passed signals at danger. The signalman at Slough East signalbox was offered the express by the signalman at Dolphin signalbox, but as the 1.5pm train was standing within his safety overlap he was unable to accept the train at 'Line Clear', but only under the warning arrangement 'Section Clear, but Station Blocked'. The signalman at Dolphin therefore kept all his signals at danger in order to caution the driver of the Falmouth express, but its driver ran past the Dolphin signals and the Slough East home signal. The driver survived the collision, but could not explain why he had passed signals at danger.

Formations: *The 1.5pm train* — four-coupled engine and tender and eight bogie coaches.
The 1.15pm train — 7ft 8in single No 3015 *Kennet* and 10 coaches (all bogies, except for one six-wheeled coach in the centre).

Damage: *The 1.5pm train* — the last two coaches were smashed, and the next two were damaged.
The 1.15pm train — the engine was damaged.

Casualties: Five passengers were killed and 35 were badly injured.

Possible safety measures: ATC would most probably have prevented this accident, and the GWR started to develop a system as a result of it.

TAPLOW
2.20am Thursday 26 October 1989

Location: Up and down relief lines. The derailment started near Milepost 23¾.

The 00.30 goods train from Whatley Quarry to Ripple Lane became derailed whilst travelling along the up relief line, and the 01.30 staff train from Paddington to Reading, travelling along the adjoining down relief line under clear signals, struck one of the derailed wagons.

Cause: A piece of wheel tread and flange had broken away from one of the wheels of the 19th wagon, caused by a fatigue crack emanating from the manufacturer's number and letter hot-stamp markings on the inside web of the wheel disc.

Formations: *The staff train* — single diesel railcar.
The goods train — diesel-electric locomotive No 56036 and 25 100-ton bogie hopper wagons loaded with stone.

Damage: *The staff train* — the railcar turned over on to its left-hand side.
The goods train — the 19th wagon was the first to derail, and all the following wagons were derailed. All except the last two turned over on to their sides.

Casualties: Nine people on the staff train received minor injuries.

Possible safety measures: More thorough examination and inspection procedures of wheelsets (subsequently adopted).

TAPLOW
approx 6.45pm Friday 8 September 1995

Location: Down main line approaching Maidenhead.

The 18.30 high-speed train from Paddington to Swansea caught fire whilst travelling at normal speed.

Cause: The rear fuel tank on the front power car became partially detached when the securing nuts unscrewed completely from the bolts, allowing the rear of the tank to drop on to the railway track. The tank was ruptured and escaping diesel fuel caught fire, the flames enveloping the exteriors of the leading coaches.

Formation: A high-speed (HST) train set, with three first class coaches leading. The train conveyed more than 550 passengers.

Damage: Mainly external fire damage.

Casualties: One passenger was killed when he jumped out of the train and was knocked down and killed by another train.

Possible safety measures: Improved methods of securing the fuel tanks, and improved maintenance schedules.

READING STATION
11.12am Wednesday 17 June 1914

Location: Up platform line.

An excursion train, the 6.32am from Taunton to Windsor, was just leaving the station and turning on to the up main line when it was in sidelong collision with the 9am express passenger train from Worcester to Paddington, which was passing through the station at about 50mph.

Cause: The driver of the excursion train passed the platform starting signal at danger. The fireman thought he saw a green flag being waved and called 'all right' to the driver. The driver, who couldn't see the platform starting signal, thought that the fireman meant that the signal had been cleared; therefore he started the train.

Formation: *The excursion train* — 4-4-0 No 3387 and nine bogie coaches.
The Worcester express — 4-4-0 No 3816 and six bogie coaches.

Damage: *The excursion train* — the engine and tender were thrown on to their sides, but none of the coaches was derailed.
The Worcester express — the engine and tender were thrown on to their sides, and all the coaches were derailed, some being damaged.

Casualties: The driver of the Worcester express was killed and both firemen were severely injured. There were no serious injuries to the passengers.

Possible safety measures: The provision of facing trap points at the end of the platform line could have minimised the effect of the platform starting signal being wrongly passed at danger.

FOXHALL JUNCTION, DIDCOT
10.41am Wednesday 27 September 1967

Location: Ladder of crossovers down relief line/up main line, and up main line/down main line, at Milepost 53¾.

The 09.45 express passenger train from Paddington to Western-super-Mare, travelling at 60-70mph, was derailed whilst being diverted from the down relief line to the down main line. The maximum permitted speed through the crossovers was 25mph.

Cause: Excessive speed.

Conditions: Fine.

Formation: 'Warship' class diesel-hydraulic locomotive No D853 *Thruster* and nine BR Mk 1 coaches. The train conveyed about 250 passengers.

Damage: The locomotive and first five coaches successfully negotiated the crossovers, but the last coach became uncoupled and fell over on to its side. The sixth, seventh and eighth coaches were derailed, and the last two turned over on to their sides.

Casualties: One passenger was killed and 23 were injured, of whom seven were detained in hospital with serious injuries.

Track layout and signalling: The down relief line ended at Foxhall Junction, but a line of rails continued straight ahead which in fact formed the termination of the up goods loop and the reception line for the power station. From the driving cab, however, it appeared that the down relief line continued straight ahead. The signalling is multiple-aspect colour-light, controlled from Reading power signalbox. The signal (R180) controlling the route from down relief to down main displayed a green aspect without route indicator when the route was set, despite the necessity to reduce speed.

Possible safety measures: It had been considered that the driver's route knowledge should be sufficient for him to be aware that a green aspect at signal R180 meant that the route ahead was set through a ladder of 25mph crossovers to the down main line, but a junction indicator was subsequently fitted to the signal as a reminder of the fact.

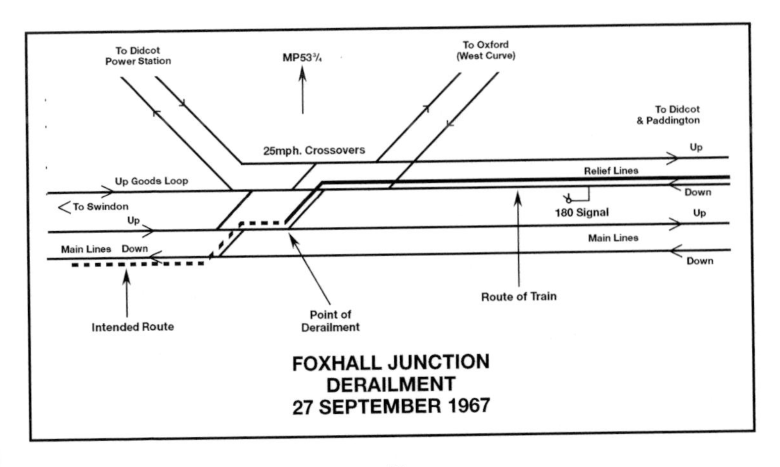

BETWEEN STEVENTON AND DIDCOT
1.15pm Sunday 20 November 1955

Location: Milton, up main line/up goods loop facing points. Between Steventon and Foxhall Junction, Didcot, just near Milepost 55¼.

The 8.30am excursion train from Treherbert to Paddington was derailed whilst being diverted to the up goods loop at Milton. The up main line ahead was blocked by planned engineering work.

Cause: Excessive speed. The train was travelling at about 50mph, and the maximum permitted speed over the points was 10mph. The driver admitted overlooking the notice of the diversion. He was also driving an engine which was relatively new to him and had lefthand drive. He admitted that he had seen neither the distant signal, which was at caution, nor the home signal, whose left-hand arm was in the clear position, indicating that the facing points were set for the goods loop. Both these signals were located to the right of the up main line. Neither driver nor fireman were alerted by the automatic train control, whose warning it is assumed that one of them re-set without realising it.

Conditions: Visibility generally good.

Formation: 'Britannia' class Pacific No 70026 *Polar Star* and 10 screw-coupled coaches. The train conveyed 293 passengers.

Damage: The engine went down a 20ft embankment and came to rest well over on its side. The first three coaches followed, the second and third being wrecked. The fourth and fifth coaches were almost completely demolished. Four more coaches were derailed.

Casualties: 11 passengers were killed and 157 were injured, of whom 62 were detained in hospital.

Possible safety measures: The drivers of passenger trains should be verbally cautioned by the signalman before entering goods loops/lines.

Right: **BETWEEN STEVENTON AND DIDCOT 20 November 1955**
The engine of the excursion train, No 70026 *Polar Star*, lies forlornly in the mud at the foot of the embankment after the high speed derailment. ***BR/IAL***

SHRIVENHAM
5.25am Wednesday 15 January 1936

Location: Up main line approx ¾-mile west of Shrivenham station.

The 9pm sleeping car express from Penzance to Paddington was running under clear signals at about 55mph, when it collided with the stationary rear portion of a 10.30pm special mineral train from Aberdare to Old Oak Common, which had broken in two. The front portion of the mineral train came to a stand at Knighton Crossing signalbox, about three miles further along the line, without the enginemen realising that the train had broken in two. The rear portion, consisting of five wagons and a brakevan, came to a stand 1,064yd west of Shrivenham signalbox.

Cause: A broken drawbar on a wagon. The signalman at Shrivenham signalbox failed to notice that the mineral train was incomplete and carried neither tail lamp nor side lamps. He therefore gave 'Train out of Section' to the signalbox in rear, Marston Crossing, and accepted the sleeping car express. The same error occurred at the next signalbox, Ashbury Crossing, therefore the signalman at Shrivenham cleared all his signals for the express. The guard of the mineral train said that he thought that the train had stopped at the home signal at Shrivenham, but several minutes later he saw the headlights of the approaching express some distance away; he had then no time to carry out the protection which he should have done sooner.

Conditions: Dark and frosty.

Formations: *The express* — 'King' class 4-6-0 No 6007 *King William III* and nine bogie vehicles, marshalled — coach, van, two sleepers, two coaches, two sleepers and a coach.

70026

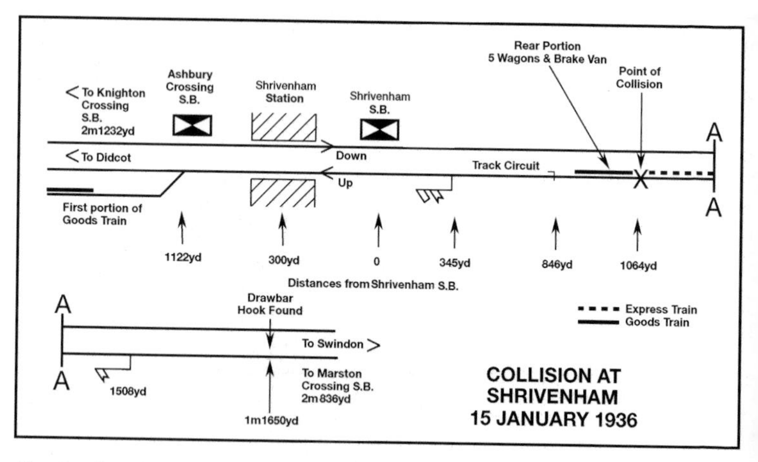

The mineral train — 2-8-0 No 2802, 53 wagons of coal and a brakevan.

Damage: *The express* — the engine turned over on to its side, and the leading coach and van were wrecked. There was some damage to the next two vehicles (sleepers).
The mineral train — several wagons were smashed.

Casualties: The driver and a passenger were killed.

Possible safety measures: This accident emphasised the importance of the signalman observing the tail lamp, and protection being carried out promptly.

THINGLEY JUNCTION, BETWEEN CHIPPENHAM AND BATH 7.12pm Wednesday 16 January 1907

Location: At the diamond crossing of the junction, where the down main line crosses the up branch line.

The 6.30pm passenger train from Westbury to Paddington via Chippenham, coming off the branch, collided engine to engine at low speed with the 5.5pm goods train from Swindon to Plymouth, running on the down main line.

Cause: The passenger train had been accepted under Block Regulation 5 (Section clear but Junction blocked) by the signalman at Thingley Junction, and the driver had been properly warned about this by the signalman at the signalbox in rear, Melksham, but the driver failed to stop at the branch home signal, which was at danger. The signalman had also accepted the goods train under Block Regulation 5, and it had already passed the distant signal at danger before the signalman decided to give it priority at the junction; therefore it was travelling quite slowly.

Conditions: Dark, but clear.

Formation: *The passenger train* — 2-4-0 engine No 70 and four bogie vehicles.
The goods train — 0-6-0 No 2448, with 43 wagons and brakevan.

Damage: *The passenger train* — the engine was not derailed, but the tender and the first coach were derailed and telescoped.
The goods train — the engine was turned over on to its side, and many wagons were derailed, some being piled up.

Above: **THINGLEY JUNCTION 16 January 1907**
'Castle' class 4-6-0 No 5023 *Brecon Castle* heads the 'Cornish Riviera Express' past Thingley Junction on 21 October 1951. The train had been diverted from its normal route owing to engineering work at Lavington.*G. J. Jefferson*

Casualties: Five passengers were injured, one seriously. The enginemen of both trains were all injured.

Signalling: Absolute block with semaphore signals. The fouling point at the diamond crossing was 54yd beyond the up branch home signal. The signalman was booked a 10hr day.

Possible safety measures: The use of Block Regulation 5 (the Warning Arrangement) for passenger trains should be restricted.

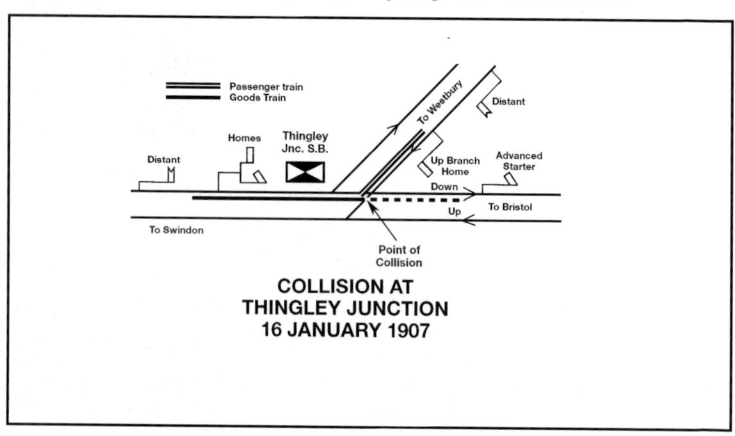

ST ANNE'S PARK, BRISTOL
2.10pm Wednesday 11 January 1967

Location: The collision occurred on the down main line between St Anne's Park Nos 2 and 3 tunnels.

The 11.45 express passenger train from Paddington to Bristol was standing at the down main line home signal at Bristol East Depot Main Line signalbox, when it was run into at the rear, at low speed, by the 12.00 express passenger train from Paddington to Swansea.

Cause: Irregular block working. The signalman at Bristol East Depot had forgotten about the Bristol train being in the rear section. He saw the block indicator showing 'Train on Line' for that section and assumed that he had forgotten to send 'Train out of Section' to the rear signalbox, Keynsham and Somerdale West, for a light engine which had passed some minutes previously. Accordingly, he cleared his block indicator and accepted the Swansea train, but did not clear his signals because he was allowing a conflicting movement ahead. The Bristol train then arrived at his home signal and was run into a few minutes later by the Swansea train, whose driver had seen the distant signal at caution and was preparing to stop at the home signal.

Conditions: Fine.

Formation: *The Bristol train* — 'Western' class diesel-hydraulic locomotive No D1067 *Western Druid* and 13 bogie vehicles. The train conveyed 204 passengers.

Right: **ST ANNE'S PARK, BRISTOL 11 January 1967**
A three-car diesel multiple-unit passes through Keynsham station on 19 June 1974 on the 12.08 Bristol to Weymouth. *G. Scott Lowe*

2B
B577

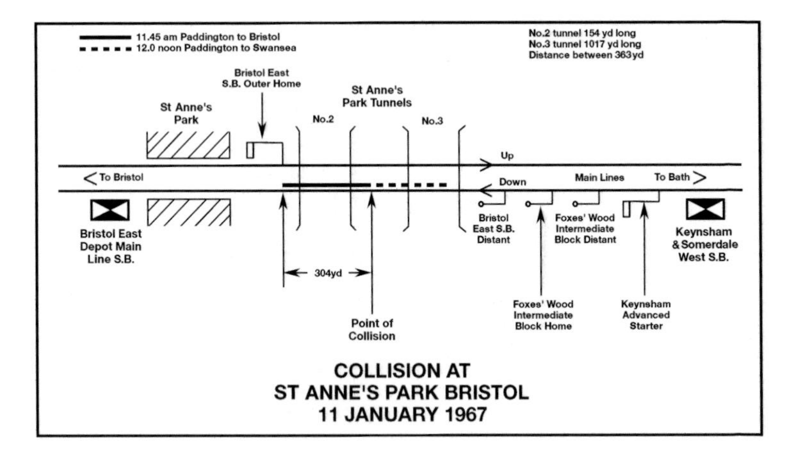

The Swansea train — 'Western' class diesel-hydraulic locomotive No D1071 *Western Renown* and 12 bogie vehicles. It conveyed 197 passengers.

Damage: The last coach (GWR design) of the Bristol train and the driving cab of the locomotive of the Swansea train were very badly damaged.

Casualties: There were no fatalities or serious injuries, although eight passengers were taken to hospital.

Signalling: Absolute block from Keynsham and Somerdale West signalbox, 2¾ miles away. There was an intermediate block section, known as Foxes Wood, on the down line. The stop signals on the down main line at Bristol East Depot were semaphores, but the distant signal was a colour-light.

Possible safety measures: Installation of 'Welwyn' control, to ensure that a second train cannot be accepted until the first train has passed through the section and has cleared the berth track circuit. It had not been the policy of the Western Region to provide these controls until 1960, after Bristol East Depot signalbox had been brought into service.

BRIDGWATER
5.4am Wednesday 23 October 1974

Location: At 151 miles 27ch on the down main line approaching Bridgwater station, approximately 400yd beyond the British Cellophane Ltd private siding connection.

The 18.28 company freight train from Ince and Elton to Bridgwater was standing on the down line at B618 position light ground signal, waiting to be put through the facing crossover on to the up main line preparatory to being set back in to Bridgwater Yard, when it was run into at the rear at about 45mph by the 19.42 Class 6 freight train from Derby to Exeter Riverside.

Cause: The Class 6 freight train had passed a colour-light signal at danger. The railway Inspecting Officer who held an inquiry had little doubt that both driver and secondman had fallen asleep.

Conditions: Dark, but fine and clear.

Formations: *The train from Ince* — diesel-electric locomotive No 47441 hauling 13 privately-owned bogie pallet vans conveying Shellstar bagged fertiliser traffic.

The train from Derby — diesel-electric locomotive No 45125 hauling 29 loaded and 13 empty wagons. Fully fitted, with the vacuum brake. Maximum permitted speed 45mph.

Damage: *The train from Ince* — the last two vehicles were telescoped and severely damaged.
The train from Derby — both cabs of the locomotive were crushed, and the following 15 wagons were derailed and piled up in confusion.

Casualties: The guard of the train from Derby was killed, and the driver and secondman were detained in hospital, but not seriously injured.

Signalling: Track circuit block regulations, worked from Bristol power signalbox, with continuous track circuiting and three-aspect colour-light signalling. Local points at Bridgwater were operated manually from a ground frame on the up platform at the station. Former GWR-type automatic train control equipment was provided at signals, but the locomotive of the train from Derby was equipped with BR standard AWS and the driver would receive no cab indications.

Possible safety measures: The conversion of ex-GWR ATC to BR AWS had already been planned for this section of line.

Postscript: The driver of the train from Derby was charged with unlawful killing, but at a hearing at Bridgwater Magistrates' Court on 28 April 1975 the case was dismissed as 'no case to answer'.

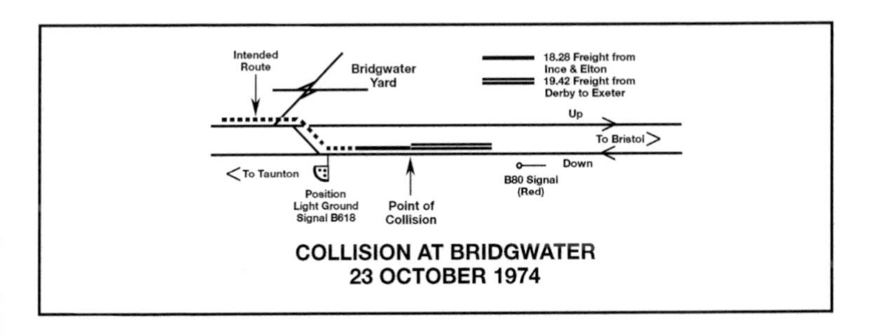

COLLISION AT BRIDGWATER
23 OCTOBER 1974

TAUNTON
2.41am Thursday 6 July 1978

Location: Up main line at Milepost 163¾, about ½-mile before Taunton station.

The 21.30 sleeping car express from Penzance to Paddington was approaching Taunton and being braked for the station stop, when fire broke out in the leading sleeping car and the communication cord was pulled.

Cause: Bags of bed linen had been placed against an electric convector heater in the vestibule of a sleeping car whilst it was standing in a bay platform at Plymouth waiting to be attached to the main train. At this time the heater was not on, but when the sleeping car was attached to the main train the heater was energised and the bags of linen began to smoulder. They finally ignited.

Conditions: Fine and dark.

Formation: Diesel-electric locomotive No 47498 and 15 vehicles, marshalled guard's brakevan, eight sleeping cars, two coaches, a guard's brakevan, two coaches and a general utility van.

Damage: The interior of the sleeping car was almost completely gutted.

Casualties: 12 passengers lost their lives (nine from carbon monoxide poisoning, two from heart attacks and one from pneumonia), and 16 were injured. Verdicts of accidental death were recorded at the Coroner's Inquest.

Possible safety measures: Better training, supervision and control of sleeping car attendants. Grilles to be fitted over wall heaters. Modifications to the construction and design of sleeping cars (adopted in the Mk 3 sleeping cars).

NORTON FITZWARREN
3.47am Monday 4 November 1940

Location: Termination of down relief line.

The 9.50pm express passenger train from Paddington to Penzance, travelling at 40-45mph, became derailed at the trap points at the termination of the down relief line where it joined the down main line, west of the station.

The driver passed Norton Fitzwarren's stop signals at danger. It is thought that he believed he was running on the down main line, for which all the signals had been cleared for a newspaper train, and he did not realise his mistake until he was almost at the end of the down relief line. Some of the signals for the down main line between Taunton and Norton Fitzwarren were on the right-hand side of the down main line and that may have led to the driver's error. He did not respond to the automatic train control warning at Norton Fitzwarren's down relief distant signal, and

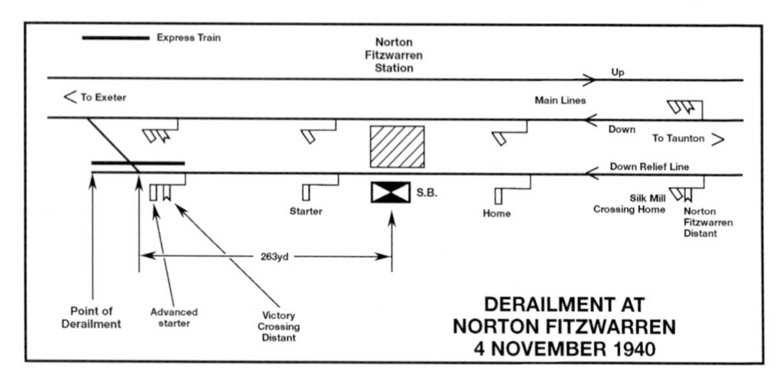

Below: **NORTON FITZWARREN 4 November 1940**
The view westwards from the station footbridge as 'King' class 4-6-0 No 6008 *King James II* approaches with an up 'West of England Express'. The coaches on the left are standing on the down relief line. *P. Poulter*

the warning detonators placed on the line by machine by the signalman at Norton Fitzwarren were too late to be effective.

Conditions: Dark and stormy.

Formation: 'King' class 4-6-0 No 6028 *King George VI* and 13 vehicles including sleeping cars. The train conveyed about 900 passengers.

Damage: The engine turned over on to its side, and the first two coaches shot past it. The third coach was partly crushed against the tender, and the fifth against the third. The fourth coach came to rest across the down main line.

Casualties: 25 passengers were killed, plus the fireman and one other railwayman. In all, 56 injured passengers were detained in hospital.

Signalling: Absolute block with semaphore signals. Automatic train control apparatus was provided. The home signal was 631yd from the trap points.

Possible safety measures: Extend the trap points with a short length of track, fitted with a sand drag.

BRADFORD ON TONE LEVEL CROSSING
Thursday 16 May 1991

Location: Between Taunton and Wellington.

A freight train conveying loaded tank wagons from Waterston (Milford Haven) to Heathfield became derailed in running, and the contents caught fire.

Cause: A collapsed axle on one of the tank wagons caused the derailment. The tank body of the fourth vehicle, containing diesel fuel, was holed by a wheel flange.

Formation: Locomotive and 22 four-wheeled tank wagons, conveying flammable liquids.

Damage: The whole train was derailed, with the first six wagons being turned on to their sides. The remaining wagons caught fire.

Casualties: None.

Possible safety measures: Stricter examination standards of privately-owned tank wagon axles.

ALLER JUNCTION
8.37am Wednesday 24 April 1929

Location: In rear of the up main line starting signal at Aller Junction.

The 5.50am goods train from Tavistock Junction to Bristol had stopped at the notice board adjoining the up main line starting signal, for the purpose of releasing the handbrakes which had been pinned down during the descent of Dainton Bank. The train was just restarting, when it was struck in the rear by the 7.10am passenger train from Plymouth to Newton Abbot, running under clear signals at 45mph.

Cause: The signalman had accepted a train from the Torquay branch and decided to run it along the up relief line. He cleared his up relief line starting signal correctly, but then unfortunately, by mistake, he cleared his up main line inner and outer home signals, instead of the relief line signals. The up main line starting signal was already in the off position for the goods train. The driver of the passenger train from Plymouth, having passed the up main line distant at caution, saw the up main line outer and inner home signals in the clear position, and proceeded on his way.

Conditions: Fine and dry.

Formations: *The passenger train* — 'Hall' class 4-6-0 No 4909 *Blakesley Hall*, a van, three bogie coaches and a van.
The goods train — 2-8-0 No 2865, 44 wagons, a crane wagon and runner, and a brakevan.

Damage: *The passenger train* — the engine was damaged, and there was slight telescoping of the first two vehicles.
The goods train — several wagons were thrown aside or otherwise damaged.

Above: **ALLER JUNCTION 24 April 1929**
The tangle of lines at Aller Junction can be seen in this photograph, as the 8.30am Plymouth to Paddington express passes, double-headed by 'Manor' class 4-6-0 No 7813 *Freshford Manor* and an unknown 'King'.
T. E. Williams/IAL

Casualties: The crane attendant, who was travelling in the brakevan, was killed. The driver and fireman of the passenger train, and seven passengers, were injured.

Signalling: Absolute block with semaphore signals.

Possible safety measures: Sequential locking would have prevented the signalman from clearing the up main line home signal when the up main line starter was already in the clear position. A track circuit in rear of the up main line starting signal, when occupied, would have prevented the up main line home signal from being cleared. Block controls on the up main line outer home signal, allowing only one release, would have prevented the signalman from clearing that signal.

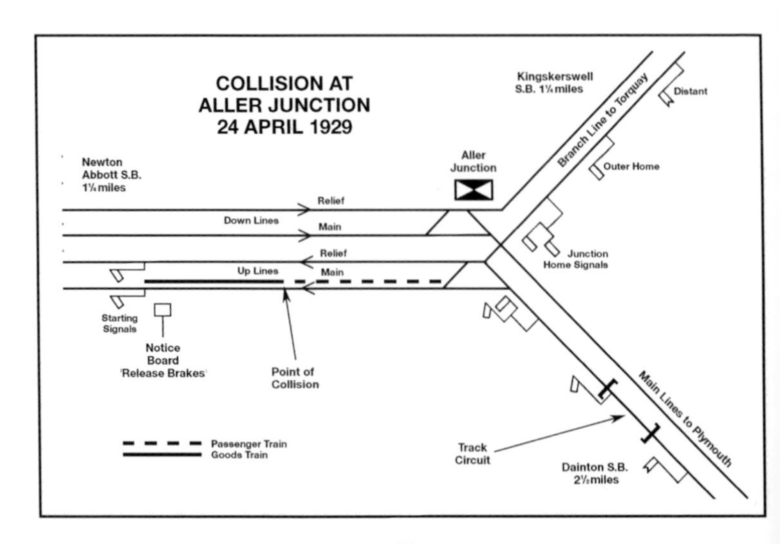

4 — South Western Main Line

Waterloo to Exeter

WATERLOO
3.35pm Thursday 5 May 1904

Location: Up Windsor line just outside the station.

The 1.45pm passenger train from Reading was entering the station on the up Windsor line into Platform 13, when it collided, engine to engine, with an empty milk train which was just being drawn out of the station from Platform 18.

Cause: The signal wire to a shunt-out signal from Platform 18 had been actuated in some manner by a signal lineman who was working in the vicinity. This caused the signal arm to move to the 'proceed' position, which led to the milk train leaving the platform.

Formation: *The passenger train* — 4-4-2T No 494 and seven eight-wheeled coaches, with a six-wheeled van at each end.
The milk train — 0-4-4T No 108.

Damage: Both engines and one coach were damaged.

Casualties: One passenger was killed and three were seriously injured.

Possible safety measures: Plans were already in existence for improving the signalling arrangements, which had been in use for many years and were open to criticism in many respects.

WATERLOO
5.26pm Tuesday 11 April 1961

Location: 195yd beyond the up main local line outer home signal on the connection to the through lines.

The 4.38pm electric multiple-unit from Effingham Junction to Waterloo approached the terminus on the up main local line and should have stopped at the outer home colour-light signal, which was showing red. However, it failed to do so, and was diverted by

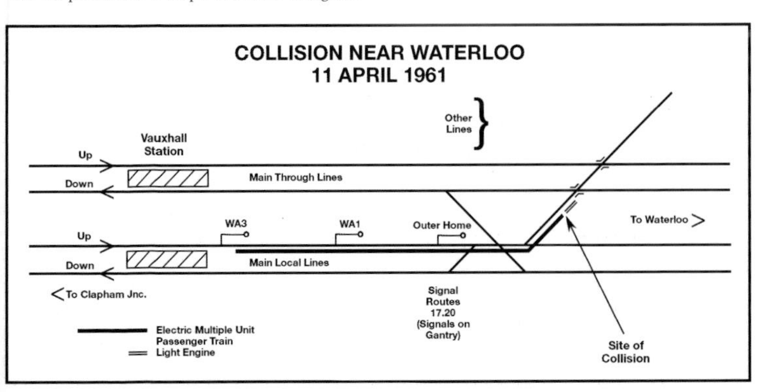

the lie of the facing points ahead into a head-on collision, at about 20-25mph, with a light engine which was passing in the down direction from the down main through line at about 12mph en route to the motive power depot.

Cause: Signal wrongly passed at danger by the passenger train.

Conditions: Fine and clear.

Formation: *The passenger train* — two four-car electric multiple-units.
The light engine — modified 'West Country' class Pacific.

Damage: The passenger train — the driving cab was wrecked and there was some telescoping between the first and second cars. The train conveyed about 100 passengers.

Casualties: The motorman of the electric train was killed.

Possible safety measures: Automatic warning signalling (AWS) would almost certainly have prevented this accident.

CLAPHAM JUNCTION
8.10am Monday 12 December 1988

Location: On the up main through line, a train's length in rear of signal WF46/47, approaching Clapham Junction station.

The driver of the 07.18 passenger train from Basingstoke to Waterloo was approaching Clapham Junction under clear signals at about 65-70mph, when signal WF138 suddenly changed from green to red when the train was close to it. The driver braked sharply, then stopped at the next signal WF46/47 in order to report the incident to the signalman, as required by the Rules. Whilst the train was standing there, it was run into in the rear, at a speed of about 35mph, by the 06.14 passenger train from Poole to Waterloo. The force of the collision diverted the Poole train towards the adjoining line, the down main through line, on which an empty train was just passing. A fourth train was approaching Waterloo on the up main through line, and its driver saw signal WF138 displaying a single yellow. He also saw the rear of the Poole train and was able to stop his train only 60yd from the rear of the Poole train.

Cause: Faulty wiring by a signal technician had

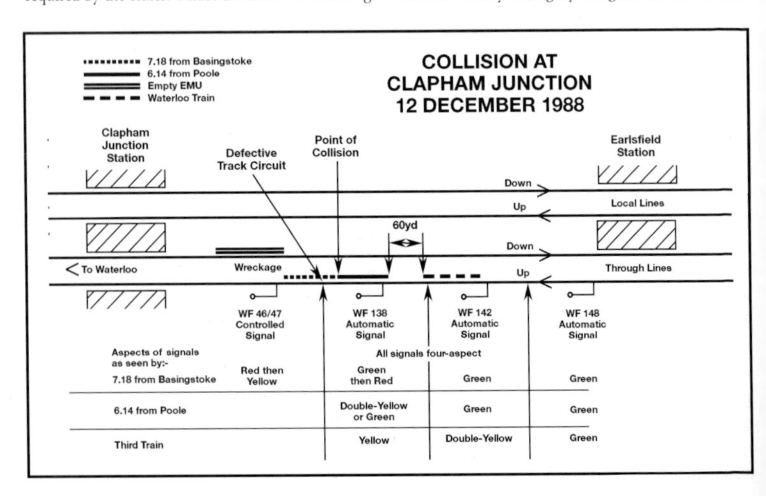

Above: **CLAPHAM JUNCTION 12 December 1988**
Clearing-up operations continue through the night. *J. de Souza*

caused a 'wrong side' failure of a track circuit. A stray wire had caused the track circuit to be energised continuously, and short-circuiting of the track circuit by the train was thus overridden and ineffective. The track circuit therefore failed to register the presence of the Basingstoke train, and consequently allowed the signal in rear, WF138, to falsely display a proceed aspect.

Formations: *The Basingstoke train* — three four-car electric multiple units. The train conveyed approximately 800 passengers.
The Poole train — three four-car electric multiple units. The train conveyed approximately 600 passengers.
The empty train — two four-car electric multiple units.

Damage: *The Basingstoke train* — the last car was thrown up on to the embankment and came to rest on its side. The next car was thrown against the retaining wall.
The Poole train — the first two cars were trapped between the two other trains and destroyed.
The empty train — several cars were derailed.

Casualties: 35 people were killed, all of whom were travelling in the first two cars of the Poole train, and 69 were seriously injured. Several hundred were less seriously injured.

Signalling: Track circuit block with continuous track circuiting and multiple-aspect colour-light signalling.

Possible safety measures: Improved procedures and supervision of wiring work. Many other recommendations were made by the Inquiry, which was a formal investigation held under Section 7 of the Regulation of Railways Act 1871. This was the first time that the powers under Section 7 had been used to hold a formal investigation into a collision between trains.

BETWEEN WIMBLEDON AND RAYNES PARK
3.25pm Thursday 25 May 1933

Location: On the down through line, ¼-mile east of Raynes Park signalbox.

The 3.10pm steam-hauled passenger train from Waterloo to Alton was passing along the down through line under clear signals, when it was completely derailed. Before it had come to a stand it was struck by the 12.11pm passenger train from Southampton Terminus to Waterloo, which was running under clear signals on the adjoining up through line.

Cause: Faulty permanent way operations. The track of the down through line was being lifted at one side in order to increase the cant, and the work was being carried out between trains. Jacks were used to lift the sleepers, which were then packed underneath to the required extent. When the Alton train came along, the jacks were removed, but several sleepers had not yet been packed and were unsupported, causing the engine to rock and derail.

Conditions: Fine and dry.

Formations: *The Alton train* — 0-4-4T No 107, travelling chimney first, and five bogie coaches. The train conveyed about 150 passengers.
The Southampton train — 2-6-0 No 1621, a bogie van and five bogie coaches. The train conveyed about 70 passengers.

Damage: *The Alton train* — the engine was derailed to the left, and all coaches were derailed. The rear of the first coach and the front of the second were derailed foul of the adjoining up through line.

The Southampton train — the engine appeared to have struck the Alton train in the middle of the first coach, but was not greatly damaged.

Casualties: Five passengers in the Alton train were killed, and three who were injured were detained in hospital. The driver of the Southampton train was seriously injured.

Possible safety measures: A temporary speed restriction should be imposed when such work is carried out on a line with a frequent service. Alternatively the line should be closed, for such work to be done at night or on Sunday.

SURBITON
10.5am Sunday 4 July 1971

Location: In the area of Surbiton station.

The 08.25 engineer's ballast train from Clapham Yard to Farnham was approaching Surbiton station at slow speed on the down slow line, when the 24th wagon, which had become buffer-locked with the 23rd, became derailed at facing points. The wagon struck the ramp of the down slow platform and, together with the following wagon, swung foul of the down fast line on which the 09.50 passenger train from Waterloo to Portsmouth Harbour was approaching at about 70mph. The passenger train struck the derailed wagons and was itself derailed.

Cause: It is probable that the buffer-locking occurred in the sidings at Clapham Yard.

Conditions: Warm and clear.

Formations: *The passenger train* — two four-car electric multiple-units.
The ballast train — Class 73 electro-diesel locomotives Nos E6025 (leading) and E6033, hauling 45 wagons with a brakevan at each end. In all, 34 of the wagons were loaded, and 11 were empty.

Damage: *The passenger train* — the first car was derailed and turned on to its side. All the other cars were derailed, except the third one.
The ballast train — the first five vehicles were derailed, some being overturned, and the 24th to the 26th were also derailed.

Casualties: Ten passengers (all in the leading car), and the driver were taken to hospital, but only three were detained.

Signalling: Track circuit block with continuous track circuiting and multiple-aspect colour-light signalling.

HAMPTON COURT JUNCTION
1.20pm Friday 23 February 1979

Location: Hampton Court Junction, up slow line.

The 13.13 passenger train from Hampton Court to Waterloo, coming off the branch on to the up slow line, collided sidelong with the rear three cars of the 12.20 from Alton/12.28 from Basingstoke to Waterloo.

Cause: The driver of the Hampton Court train had wrongly passed the junction signal at danger.

Conditions: Dry, with bright sunshine.

Formations: *The Hampton Court train* — two four-car electric multiple-units.
The Alton/Basingstoke train — two four-car electric multiple-units.

Damage: *The Hampton Court train* — the leading car was diverted down a steep embankment and the second car was damaged.
The Alton/Basingstoke train — the last three cars suffered external damage.

Casualties: Several people were taken to hospital, but none was detained.

Signalling: Track circuit block with continuous track circuiting and multiple-aspect colour-light signalling. The signals were equipped with AWS.

Possible safety measures: The Hampton Court train was not equipped with AWS, but was subsequently dealt with.

ESHER
8.23pm Sunday 28 January 1945

Location: Down through line at Esher station.

The 7.48pm passenger train from Waterloo to Bournemouth had been stopped at Esher down home signal, and was gathering speed again after the signal had been cleared. It had reached approx 30mph, when it was run into in the rear by the 7.57pm electric passenger train from Waterloo to Portsmouth, which was running under clear signals at about 50mph.

Cause: It was assumed to have been the incorrect use of the release key for the Lock and Block signalling equipment by the signalman at Esher signalbox, although the signalman at the previous signalbox, Hampton Court Junction, should have

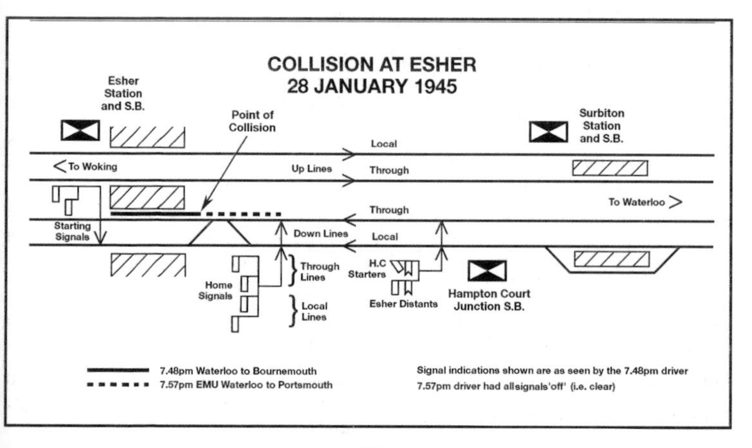

noticed irregularities in the block instrument indications and bell signals.

Conditions: Clear, cold and dark, with snow lying.

Formations: *The Bournemouth train* – 'King Arthur' class 4-6-0 No 785 *Sir Mador de la Porte* and 13 bogie vehicles.
The Portsmouth train — four two-car electric multiple-units.

Damage: The electric train suffered some telescoping between the first and second cars.

Casualties: One passenger in the electric train was killed, and 19 injured passengers were taken to hospital.

Signalling: Sykes Lock and Block with semaphore signals.

Possible safety measures: Plans to install colour-light signalling and continuous track circuiting had been postponed by the war.

Postscript: A short time earlier (a few weeks?) an enemy missile (a V2 rocket) fell near Hampton Court Junction signalbox and severely damaged it. Also, the first thoughts of the driver of the steam train when he felt the jolt of the collision were that it had been caused by a V2 rocket.

Above: **ESHER 28 January 1945**
Looking east from Walton-on-Thames station, the 11.54am Waterloo to Salisbury is seen approaching on the down through line on 11 November 1950, headed by 'Merchant Navy' class Pacific No 35006 *Peninsular and Oriental. S. N. Co. E. D. Bruton/IAL*

WOKING
8.29pm Wednesday 23 December 1955

Location: A train's length in rear of Woking down through line home signal.

The 7.50pm electric multiple-unit passenger train from Waterloo to Portsmouth had been standing for a few minutes at Woking down through line home signal when it was struck at the rear at low speed by the 7.54pm steam-hauled passenger train from Waterloo to Basingstoke. The bogie of the last coach of the Portsmouth train was thrown foul of the adjoining up through line, and an up passenger train just starting from Woking scraped past it, but was not derailed.

Cause: The driver of the Basingstoke train ran past Maybury down through line intermediate block home signal at danger.

Conditions: Fine and clear, but dark.

Formations: *The 7.50pm Portsmouth* — three

Above: **WOKING 23 December 1955**
Southern Railway 'Merchant Navy' class Pacific No 35007 *Aberdeen Commonwealth* at West Weybridge on a train of milk tanks. Date unknown. *E. R. Wethersett/IAL*

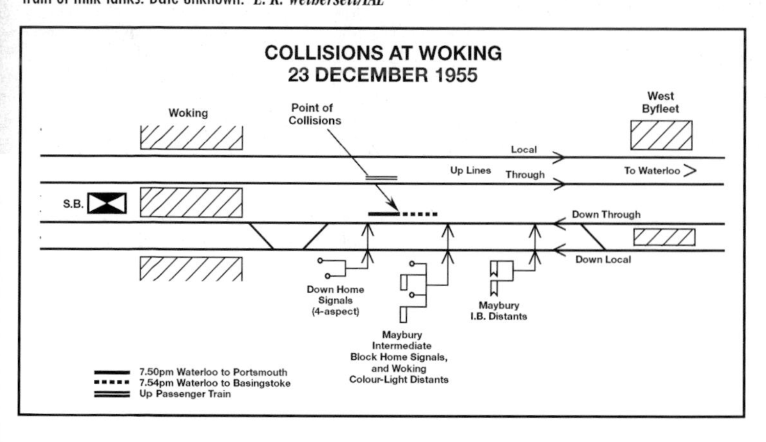

four-car electric multiple-units.
The 7.54pm Basingstoke — 'Remembrance' class 4-6-0 and eight coaches.

Damage: The rear of the last car of the 7.50pm train was crushed.

Casualties: Some minor injuries.

Signalling: Sykes Lock and Block between West Byfleet and Woking. There was an intermediate block section, known as Maybury, which used semaphore signals, but underneath the home signals there were located Woking's distant signals, which were of the colour-light type, and it was thought that the brighter yellow light displayed by the colour-light distant may have masked the lower-intensity red light of the home signal.

Possible safety measures: Automatic warning signalling (AWS) would have prevented this accident. The design of Maybury's home signals, combining both a semaphore and a colour-light signal, could have been improved by combining both indications in a three- or four-aspect colour-light signal and abolishing the semaphore arms. A brighter tail lamp on the 7.50pm train might have helped the driver of the 7.54pm train to pick it out earlier.

FARNBOROUGH
6.5pm Wednesday 26 November 1947

Location: Up through line, a short distance west of Farnborough station at signal WA113.

The 3.5pm express passenger train from Bournemouth West to Waterloo had been waiting for several minutes at a failed automatic signal WA113, when it was run into in the rear by the 12.15pm express passenger train from Ilfracombe to Waterloo.

Cause: The electric power supply to the signals had failed, and the signalman had issued an instruction to the driver of the Ilfracombe train to ignore certain automatic signals without first going through the procedure for establishing emergency block working and ascertaining that the section concerned was unoccupied.

Conditions: Fine, clear and cold.

Formations: *The Bournemouth train* — 'Lord Nelson' class 4-6-0 No 860 *Lord Hawke* and 10 bogie vehicles.
The Ilfracombe train — 'King Arthur' Class N15 4-6-0 No 453 *King Arthur*

Damage: *The Bournemouth train* — the last two vehicles were demolished.

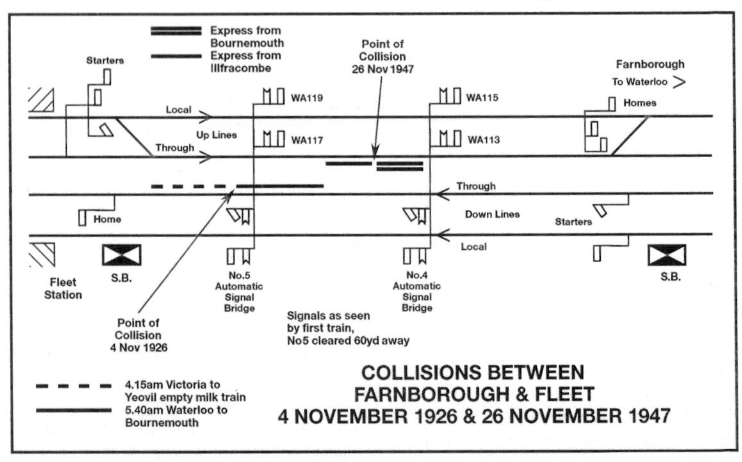

COLLISIONS BETWEEN FARNBOROUGH & FLEET 4 NOVEMBER 1926 & 26 NOVEMBER 1947

The Ilfracombe train — the engine was overturned.

Casualties: One passenger was killed and a railwayman on duty was fatally injured.

Signalling: Low pressure automatic signalling between Fleet and Farnborough.

Possible safety measures: Improve the telephone arrangements from the automatic signals to the controlling signalmen.

BETWEEN FARNBOROUGH AND FLEET
6.39am Thursday 4 November 1926

Location: On the down through line, approx one mile east of Fleet station.

The 4.15am empty milk train from Victoria to Yeovil came to a stand about a train length beyond No 5 automatic signal bridge owing to a drawbar hook fracturing and causing the train to break into two. The following train, the 5.40am express from Waterloo to Bournemouth and Weymouth, passed a signal at danger and crashed into the milk train at not less than 40mph.

Cause: The drawbar was thought to have broken when the driver reapplied steam after being brought almost to a stand at No 5 automatic signal. The milk train stood for about 8min whilst the train crew tried to recouple the two portions, but the guard of the milk train should have started to protect his train and should have telephoned the Farnborough signalman from No 5 signal bridge. Had he done so, the accident might have been prevented. However, the main cause was the driver of the express wrongly passing No 5 automatic stop signal at danger.

Conditions: Damp and misty. Not yet daylight.

Formation: The express — 'King Arthur' class 4-6-0 No E452 *Sir Meliagrance* and 13 vehicles.

Damage: *The express* — the engine turned over on to its side, and the first three vehicles were derailed. *The milk train* — the rear 10 vehicles were destroyed.

Casualties: The driver of the express was killed.

Signalling: Low-pressure electro-pneumatic automatic signalling between Farnborough and Fleet, with semaphore signals. Installed in 1905. Track circuited throughout. Distant signals still showed a red light for caution at this location.

Possible safety measures: Automatic train control (ATC) would have prevented this collision.

SALISBURY
1.57am Sunday 1 July 1906

Location: Up through line at the east end of the station.

The weekly boat express from Plymouth to London was passing through Salisbury at 60-65mph under clear signals, when the engine and coaches left the rails and came into contact with a milk train moving in the opposite direction on the down through line and a light engine standing in the down bay platform.

Cause: Excessive speed over the curve at the east end of the station, which had a speed restriction of 30mph.

Formation: 6ft 7in 4-4-0 No 421 and five bogie vehicles marshalled guard's brakevan, three first class saloons and a kitchen brakevan, conveying 43 first class passengers who had landed at Plymouth Stonehouse Pool from the America Line ship SS New York.

Damage: The engine turned over on to its side, and the first four vehicles were wrecked.

Casualties: 24 passengers, the driver and fireman of the boat train, another fireman and a guard were killed. Seven passengers were severely injured.

Possible safety measures: There was little that could be done in those days, but distant signals fixed at caution and emergency detonator placing machines might have helped.

Postscript: Major Pringle, who held the official inquiry, said that there had been no other case of overturning caused by high speed. He also said that only two passengers had been killed on the London & South Western Railway in the last 17 years.

For all your transport requirements, visit the Ian Allan Bookshops in Birmingham, Manchester or London.

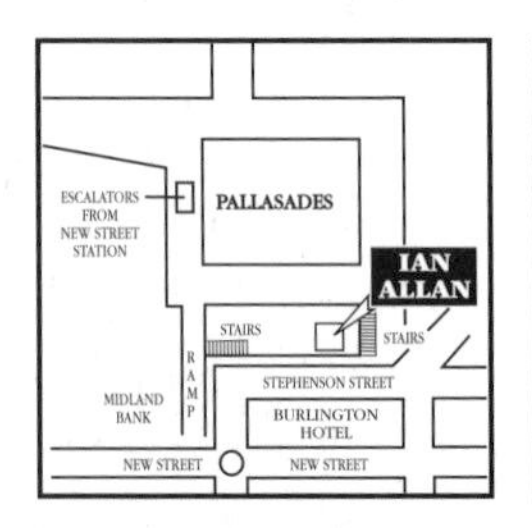

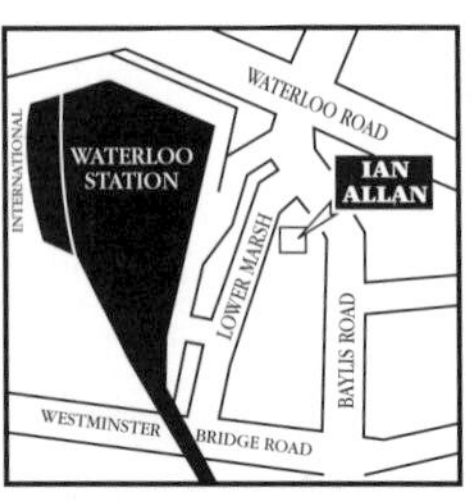

BIRMINGHAM

Unit 84
47 Stephenson Street
Birmingham B2 4DH
Tel: 0121 643 2496
Fax: 0121 643 6855

LONDON

45/46 Lower Marsh
Waterloo
London SE1 7SG
Tel: 0171 401 2100

MANCHESTER

Unit 5
Piccadilly Station Approach
Manchester M1 2GH
Tel: 0161 237 9840
Fax: 0161 237 9921

Each shop stocks a comprehensive range of books, magazines, videos, models, badges, postcards, calendars and much more!

For the full range of Ian Allan products plus books and videos from specialist publishers large and small - call into an Ian Allan Bookshop TODAY!

The Ian Allan Bookshops also offer a mail order service - please call for details.

To find out if an Ian Allan Bookshop is opening near you, please telephone: **0161 237 9840.**